THE
HOME
BUYER'S
INSPECTION
GUIDE

James
Madorma

BETTERWAY PUBLICATIONS, INC.
WHITE HALL, VIRGINIA

Published by Betterway Publications, Inc.
P.O. Box 219
Crozet, VA 22932
(804) 823-5661

Cover design by Deborah B. Chappell
Typography by East Coast Typography, Inc.

Every precaution has been taken in preparing *The Home Buyer's Inspection Guide* to make this book as complete and accurate as possible. Neither the author nor Betterway Publications, Inc., however, assume any responsibility for any damages or losses incurred in conjunction with the use of this guide.

The following names used in this book are registered trademarks: Freon®, Sheetrock®.

Library of Congress Cataloging-in-Publication Data

Madorma, James
    The home buyer's inspection guide / James Madorma.
        p. cm.
    Includes bibliographical references.
    ISBN 1-55870-146-X : $11.95
        1. Dwellings—Inspection.   2. House buying.   I. Title.
TH4817.5.M33   1990
643'.12—dc20   89-18323
                                                            CIP

Printed in the United States of America
0 9 8 7 6 5 4 3 2 1

This book is dedicated to my wife,
Marie Avona Madorma,
whose skills as an editor made its publication possible.

Preface

This book is not being written just to tell a prospective home buyer how to inspect the property by himself or herself. There are books already available to do that. Instead, this book has been written to make the home buyer aware of problems that could eventually arise in the future due to existing conditions. Often people will still buy a house with these potential problems because the price is low, the style of the house is special, the area is convenient, or for a combination of these reasons. Potential problems are not reasons to forgo a purchase if, and only if, you have been prepared to deal with them.

I bought an old house that had not been maintained because I knew that the structure was sound, renovation was not impossible and that, ultimately, I'd be happy with it. It helped that the house was below market prices and it was located in a pretty area. Once the house was fixed, I knew I would have a strong, attractive old house in a convenient location. I still do, as a matter of fact.

In spite of this, I often tell my clients not to buy an old house but to buy something newer with low maintenance and few surprises. These people either cannot or simply do not want to deal with renovations or high maintenance. Ultimately, home buying is a very personal experience. The important thing is to know in advance what you're buying so that your house doesn't become a nightmare. This book should make homeownership pleasant and its surprises very few.

Each of the chapters will tell you what to look for that's good about the house you're inspecting and what could go wrong with it. Then it will provide general maintenance tips and ways to prevent problems before they occur to help the homeowner avoid high-cost repairs later. High costs that are unavoidable also will be discussed so that the home buyer will know in advance what he or she is getting into before the bills arrive. This book was written for the layman; however, it is technical enough to cover important topics. Illustrations throughout the book will make written explanations clearer. The glossary and bibliography at the end will provide additional knowledge. And, of course, the summaries and the checklists will make your job as a home inspector easier and ultimately, more efficient.

Contents

Introduction

This book has been written to take some of the panic out of home buying and its inevitable result, homeownership. That's why it will not only teach you how to inspect a house, but it also will offer enough information to prepare you for problems that could arise in the future. It was written for you, the layman, not for an architect or engineer, therefore, its explanations are clear, precise, and thorough. Illustrations throughout the book assist you in understanding its advice.

No matter what you intend to spend, or how big you intend to buy, purchasing a house is one of the most expensive things you'll do in your lifetime. Cost will vary by neighborhood and size of property, but the steps you must take to inspect it are the same, no matter how often you repeat them during the inspection. Inspections take anywhere from forty minutes to 2½ hours, depending upon the condition and size of the property. Take whatever time you need to do the inspection completely because this is something that shouldn't be rushed. If the owner doesn't want to give you the time you need for this inspection, forget the property and look for something else. Don't buy a house unless you've inspected it. Period.

There's no right or wrong kind of house to buy. You may want to buy an old house because of its charm, or a new one because of its modern design. The age of the property has little to do with anything but your taste. What concerns you are the basic structure and the various systems in that structure. You want to know their condition to be sure you know what you're getting into before mortgage payments are due. Often people buy a house that needs a lot of work and that's fine, if you're prepared to handle the work or to pay someone else to do it. Even new homes sometimes need additional features, so purchasing a new home doesn't necessarily mean that there will be no extra costs afterward. Again, that's fine too, as long as you're prepared for these costs.

This book is going to make you aware of what will definitely have to be taken care of and what you might want to do to improve the house you want to buy. This might mean that you will want to live with an old boiler for a year before you modernize it, but you must know for sure that the boiler will last one more year after you've purchased the house. It might simply suggest that you change the air valves on the radiators to improve heating the rooms, an inexpensive item you can do right away. Some problems that it may help you find, however, may be so bad that it's best not to purchase the property. Other problems may require specialized information from an electrician, plumber, or engineer. Concerns about the foundation, for instance, are reasons to call in a professional engineer rather than trying to figure them out on your own. Errors in judgment in this case could be totally devastating to you and your financial situation. This book covers many of the possible problems that you might face as a home buyer so that you are well-prepared as a homeowner.

To do this inspection right, make an appointment for this inspection with the owner and/or realtor. You definitely want to do this inspection in the daytime and, if possible, after a recent rainfall. Do not try to do this inspection at night when at least half of what you need to examine is not clearly visible. Dress down for this inspection since you'll probably get dirty on this job. Wear comfortable clothes and shoes that protect your feet from dirt, water, etc. Bring along a high-beam flashlight, not a low-beam, because you'll need to see well in dark corners and crevices, where some big problems often hide. Bring binoculars with you because they too will give you visual access to areas that have problems you otherwise might not see. You'll need to bring along two kinds of screwdrivers, Phillips and blade-head, long-handled if possible. These will be handy for checking electrical boxes and wood framing members. Bring a magnet with you to check for galvanized plumbing. This may be harder to do, but if possible, a ladder is a good item to bring to an inspection for access to roofs, attics, etc., although it's not absolutely necessary. Of course, take along a pen and something to write on, such as a notebook, in order to list items you're concerned about for discussion after the inspection is done. You should bring this book, so that you don't forget anything, and to use as a reference when viewing the house. And, of course, bring your checklist too.

There is one other essential item to take with you on this inspection and it's called tact. When you ask the owner questions about the house, do it in a friendly, conversational tone, not belligerently. After all, you want an honest answer, not an antagonistic one that you provoked. The house you're inspecting is the owner's dream house so don't criticize how it is cared for or decorated. Do-it-yourself projects in the home may have been poorly crafted but they were done with the heart, and if you make fun of the work, you've made an instant enemy out of the owner. The answers and comments you will get from that moment on will not make this inspection a thorough one. Even if you find major problems or building code violations, keep the relationship calm by making note of them in passing. Discuss them later in private with the realtor and your lawyer, then afterwards if necessary with the owner, if you decide you'd still like to purchase the house. And when you can compliment somebody's work or taste, always do so. This will make the inspection friendlier and, ultimately, more effective.

There are a few other things to remember about an inspection. You should use caution when inspecting items that could hurt you in some way. Electrical boxes should be inspected with care as well as boilers and chimneys which can be harmful. Note the items in this book which stress caution and be extra careful when you get to them during the inspection. Be alert while walking on roofs or in attics, or when crawling into a tight space. And, of course, don't damage the property in order to inspect it. That's an absolute no-no. If an area looks dangerous, don't go into it or step on it. Be careful not to fall over debris left in basements or attics, or over dead branches or shrubs in gardens. You don't want to get injured while doing this inspection just as much as you don't want to damage the property that you fall on.

When the inspection is done, you may want to think before you speak — an old but wise saying. Take time after the inspection to discuss the house's pros and cons with your spouse, the realtor, and your attorney before you decide to purchase the house. List what it will cost to fix what must be fixed; then you can determine later who will bear these costs. Sometimes all or part of the costs will come off the asking price, other times costs are shared among the owner, realtor, and/or buyer. Be aware of the fact that once the owner has decided to sell this property, that owner has very little interest in repairing it unless he or she really wants to sell it and there's no other way to do it. There are even instances where costs are so prohibitive that you will want to forget about purchasing the house altogether.

Consider all of these options before making a final decision. Just remember it is you who will pay the mortgage for the house you've purchased so don't be rushed by owners, realtors, lawyers, spouses, friends, etc. This is too big a decision to make in haste. By the same token, don't let others make this decision for you. You may be happy to solve all sorts of problems in a particular house because it's really what you're looking for, so decide for yourself. In any case, before signing any legal documents or loan agreements, secure an attorney who knows real estate law and can fully protect your rights. This book deals with engineering concerns. You need a knowledgeable real estate lawyer to deal with legal and financial matters to avoid such problems.

The last word about the inspection deals with what should not concern you. Appliances such as refrigerators, washing machines, etc., should not count for much in an inspection. This also is true of a broken screen, or a door that doesn't close tightly. These kinds of details really add very little to the purchase price of a house. Over the years you'll eventually be replacing the appliances and you'll fix the screen. They're not permanent or even essential parts of the structure, and it is the structure and its systems that you're inspecting and, finally, purchasing.

Sometimes people lose sight of the larger picture because they inspect items that are unimportant and forget to examine those that are absolutely essential. Don't win the battle and lose the war, another old saying that works well here. If the owner adamantly refuses to fix the broken screen, so be it, just so long as the house is well-built and its systems are in good working condition. Don't let the house slip out of your hands because of small maintenance items that either can be negotiated, or even cared for later by you. Once the house is yours, you'll get to the things that are important, live well anyway with those that are not, and eventually make the whole house your very own. If you inspect it carefully and decide knowledgeably, which this book will help you do, and finally, choose the house you really like, you will have purchased your perfect house, where you will live happily ever after. Now, let's start that inspection.

SUMMARY

Cost will vary by neighborhood and size of property. Inspection will take from forty minutes to 2½ hours, depending upon condition and size. Take your time and don't purchase if you can't inspect.

Buy an old or new house with little or lots of work so long as you please yourself. Sometimes new houses need work, too. You need to know if problems are too costly or difficult to solve, or if you can live with them for awhile and fix later.

Make an appointment with owner and/or realtor for the daytime, never at night, and if possible after rainfall. Dress to get dirty. Bring high-beam flashlight, binoculars, Phillips and blade-head screwdrivers, magnet, ladder, notebook, pen, and this book. Checklist, too.

Bring tact. Ask friendly, conversational questions, try to compliment homeowner to get honest answers. Don't discuss problems immediately with owner, wait to talk to realtor and/or lawyer privately.

Use caution when checking electrical boxes, boilers, chimneys, on roofs, in tight spaces, around debris, in gardens. Don't damage the property during the inspection.

Discuss pros and cons with spouse, realtor, attorney. Owner may not want to fix anything now. Costs may prohibit purchasing.

Consider all options. Don't be rushed to decide. Have attorney protect your rights.

Don't be concerned with appliances or minor problems. Structure and its systems are essential parts that you are purchasing.

Be flexible but also cautious, if you want the house. Don't lose it because of unimportant items, but don't overlook those items that are important.

1
Systems

HEATING SYSTEMS

One of the most important systems in a house is the heating system. It may be a steam, hot water, or forced-air system and it may be gas, oil, or electricity fired (see illustrations A, B, and C). The hot water may be produced in the boiler, or by a gas, oil, or electrically fired domestic hot water heater. You need to know the type of system and what type of fuel is being used for heating before buying any house.

Conversion Boiler

If an older house is being inspected, you may find the original boiler but, more than likely, you'll find a conversion type boiler in which coal was the original heating fuel but it was changed to gas or oil-fired. If it has been converted, it's probably an older, low-efficiency boiler and its size is massive compared to today's compact units. Ask the owner the age of the boiler because the efficiency of older boilers is usually between fifty and sixty percent while modern boilers are eighty to ninety percent efficient. Some of the newest boilers actually are in the ninety plus percent efficiency range these days.

Be sure to check the fire box if you're inspecting an older boiler that has been converted. In the conversion type boilers, the gas or oil-fired gun fires into a brick-lined fire box (see illustration AA). A good way to judge the age and reliability of a boiler of this type is to determine how sound the bricks are that line the fire box. Look at the fire bricks with a flashlight. If they're broken, crumbling, or loose, they will have to be repaired and/or replaced. Check to see if the fire box is clean. This can indicate whether or not the boiler has been maintained properly. Never put your hands into the boiler to inspect the fire bricks, and when you're viewing it, be sure the boiler has been completely shut off and allowed to cool. Don't even attempt to view it if the boiler has been working, or even if it was just shut off. Severe injury will result from a careless examination of the fire box in the boiler, so please be very, very careful when you look at it.

Steam Heating System

Of the three basic kinds of heating systems available, the steam system (one-pipe) is the oldest (see illustration A). After the house has been heated with steam, condensate returns through this one-pipe system back into the boiler. On the other hand, the advantage of having the hot water heating system is that after the boiler has heated the house, the hot water remains in the radiators, continuing to give off heat into the rooms for an extended period of time (see illustration B). In to-day's home construction market, however, the forced-air system is preferred because of its lower construction costs (see illustration C). It is based on a furnace/blower which distributes hot air through a system of ducting throughout the house in order to heat it. The most popular advantage of a forced-air system over the other two heating systems to the homeowner is that central air conditioning can be operated through the same ducting that is being used for heating (see illustration D).

When inspecting steam or hot water heating systems, always look around the base of the boiler for water stains as well as for water on the floor. This water and these water stains can indicate that there may be a leak or a crack in the internal section of the boiler and that water is being lost through it. They also can indicate that the gauge glass is broken. This gauge glass must be repaired immediately before the boiler is put into operation again. A leak in a section of the boiler means that a new boiler may have to be installed right away. Look at the outer cover of the boiler for signs of corrosion since this may indicate that the boiler is old and that a new boiler is going to have to be installed shortly.

Ask the owner to put the boiler into operation while you're present. Usually this is done by turning the wall thermostat up to fire the boiler. If the boiler goes on when the thermostat is raised, you know that both the boiler and the thermostat are in working condition. While the boiler is operating, throw the shut-off switch that is attached to the boiler to see if the boiler shuts off. Put the boiler back on and throw the emergency shut-off switch to be sure that it shuts the boiler off, too. Some localities require the emergency shut-off switch as a backup to the shut-off switch attached to the boiler. Be sure that a pressure safety valve is connected to the boiler. This safety valve prevents pressure buildup in the boiler. If the pressure is not relieved by the safety valve, it could cause an explosion, or even rupture the boiler.

All boilers will last longer and work more effi-ciently if they are flushed and cleaned annually. Ask the owner what he or she does to maintain the boiler. Usually a licensed plumber or the utility company provides this kind of maintenance service. Look to see if a service tag is attached to the boiler. This tag lists the dates on which the boiler was serviced and what repairs were performed.

Take a little extra time at this point in the inspection to leave the boiler in operation for ten to fifteen minutes. Make sure that the boiler flue pipe is exhausting properly to the chimney. If the chimney is clogged or partially obstructed, you can feel a great deal of heat around the boiler area. This heat is due to hot flue gases backing up into the house, instead of going up into the chimney and out into the air. This hot flue gas is carbon monoxide and it can be very dangerous if it is not vented out of the house completely. If flue gases are not vented out of the chimney, the boiler should be shut off immediately and the area vented. Tell the owner to have the utility company or a plumber check the chimney for obstructions. Tell the owner that the boiler should not be turned back on until these obstructions have been cleared.

While the boiler is operating, check to see that the cement that covers the opening between the flue pipe and the chimney wall is tightly sealed. Sometimes sections of the cement are cracked or broken away. These sections are going to have to be re-sealed to prevent any leakage of the flue gas back into the house. Carbon monoxide is a deadly gas, so you always want to be sure that it's being kept out of the house. If you see walls that are "sweating" (dampness on the walls) and/or feel a great deal of heat around the area where the boiler is located, these are indications that carbon monoxide may be present. If you ever encounter this condition as a homeowner, use your emergency switch to shut off the boiler, vent the house, and call your utility company or a plumber immediately.

Oil-Fired Heating System

In an oil-fired heating system, the fuel oil is turned into a fine spray and mixed with air by the oil-burner gun. While you are inspecting this kind of heating system, you should look at this oil-burner gun to see if it is the latest technology available on the market. Ask the owner if the oil-burner gun has ever been replaced.

Electricity-Fired Heating System

If the heating system that you're inspecting is an electrically fired forced-air system, the heat will be produced as soon as the owner adjusts the heating thermostat. A flue pipe is not required for this type of heating system because there is no need to vent flue gases up the chimney. All wiring for an electrically fired furnace must comply with the local electrical code as well as with the National Electrical Code. When inspecting an electrically fired forced-air system, get an idea of where the furnace is located in the house. The furnace should be centrally located in the house so that the ducts which supply heat throughout the house can be as short as possible. Shorter ducts will reduce heat loss in the house.

Heat Pump

If the house that you're examining is heated by a heat pump, that same heat pump can both heat and cool the house. The principle of the heat pump is that the pump takes heat from the outside climate in order to warm the house. When cooling is required, the pump removes heat and discharges it to the outside climate. In other words, a heat pump operates in the same way your household refrigerator does.

Gas-Fired Heating System

If you're inspecting a gas-fired forced-air heating system, take the front cover of the furnace off to look at the heat exchanger while the furnace is operating. Look to see if any section of the heat exchanger is cracked or damaged. If there is any damage, tell the owner to shut the system off immediately because this is a dangerous condition. Advise the owner that he must have it repaired

before it is put back into operation. In this type of heating system, the burner flame is in a chamber below the heat exchanger. Upon firing, the heat from the combustion heats the metal walls of the heat exchanger. Air flowing through the heat exchanger is being heated from its metal walls. This air flow should be uniform across the heat exchanger in order to have proper heat transfer reaction. If the volume of air is not uniform, a section of the heat exchanger may fail. If the furnace is not functioning properly and if there is a low volume of air over a section of the heat exchanger, the temperature in the heat exchanger wall will build up and cause it to fail. Look again at the combustion section and see if flames from the burner are heating the bottom of the heat exchanger. These flames should be centered in each section of the heat exchanger. If they are not centered, a section of the heat exchanger may be overheating.

Radiant Floor Heating

I've inspected a few homes in which radiant floor heating was installed, mostly in rooms where it was not possible to place radiators, baseboard heating, etc. I've also seen this system used in an addition to a house, usually an addition that was built on a concrete slab and did not have a basement. In a radiant floor heating system, tubing has been laid down in a pattern over gravel, or on a wood subfloor. The older systems used copper or steel tubing which had soldered and braised connections in it to provide an uninterrupted flow for the heated water. In homes where gravel was used as the base, a concrete slab was poured over the tubing. In cases where a wood subfloor was used as a base, a finished wood floor was installed over the tubing. Usually a finished wood floor also was installed over the concrete slab. No matter what base was used, however, great care had to be taken to make sure that the tubing was not damaged while the concrete was installed or a finished wood floor was nailed down over it.

If you are inspecting a house with radiant floor heating, ask the owner the age of the system. If it was installed about twenty-five years ago, the tubing is probably copper or steel tubing. These copper or steel tubes carry the hot water used for heating. In many of the older radiant floor heating systems, this water was heated to a temperature of between 120 and 140 degrees Fahrenheit. Today's newer systems only heat the water to 80 to 100 degrees Fahrenheit. This hot water flowing in the tubing sends heat up through the floor and provides for a comfortable heating arrangement in the room.

If you find this kind of system, what you should be concerned about is that it may have a limited life expectancy because of its age and the presence of copper or steel tubing. Usually leaks will start to develop in the tubing within twenty-five years after installation. The problem is that the combination of dissimilar metals at the tubing's joints, along with the presence of lime and moisture in the concrete, is highly corrosive and leaks will develop in the tubing at these joints. Leaks also can develop when cracks in the concrete slab rupture the tubing. Another source of trouble in these older systems with higher operating temperatures is that a wood floor can buckle or warp from the heat if it has not been installed properly. If you buy a house with an older radiant floor heating system, you may have to deal with an expensive repair bill if any of these problems occur in the future. Today's new radiant floor heating systems use polybutylene tubing instead of copper or steel tubing to eliminate any problems associated with corrosion (see illustration BB).

DOMESTIC HOT WATER HEATER

When looking at the heating system, you also should check to see if a domestic water heater is in use. It may be gas, oil, or electrically fired (see illustrations E and F). If a domestic hot water heater is not in use, then domestic hot water is being produced by a coil in the boiler. If the boiler is producing hot water, then this means that the whole boiler must fire in order to heat water for domestic use. This is a waste of fuel and it is putting an extra strain on the boiler. When a domestic hot water heater is in use, the boiler does not have to fire to heat water. The hot water heater functions all year to heat water. This heater uses less fuel and results in lower annual fuel costs for operating the house.

Despite all of these advantages, many of the homes that I've inspected continue to produce hot water utilizing the coil mechanism in the boiler. To examine the condition of the coil mechanism, remove the cover from the front of the boiler. If you see water stains or rust spots around the area where the coil mechanism is inserted into the boiler, these are tip-offs to a potential problem with the coil. When the coil fails, as they eventually all do, I recommend that a domestic hot water heater be installed instead of a new coil (see illustrations CC and DD).

Ask the owner the age of the domestic hot water heater. The life expectancy of a gas or oil-fired domestic hot water heater averages approximately ten years.

On the front of the domestic hot water heater there's usually a metal tag at the base of the heater, near the ignition controls. Look at this tag to find out the capacity of the hot water heater in gallons and the recovery rate in gallons-per-hour. The recovery rate indicates how many gallons of hot water this unit can heat in one hour.

It is important to ask the seller if this unit has ever been drained or flushed. Draining and flushing a unit increases its life-expectancy. Also look to see if a pressure safety valve has been installed. There should be a pipe connected from the pressure safety valve, running down the side of the unit and ending a short distance off the floor. The purpose of this valve and pipe is to relieve the internal pressure buildup in the tank which can occur if the unit is not operating properly. If this pressure is not relieved, the tank can explode or rupture. It has even been known to take off through the house like a rocket with just about as much damage. To prevent this dangerous condition, the safety valve opens to release scalding water and steam when pressure has built up in the tank. If no pipe is running down the side of the tank, this scalding water and steam can seriously injure anyone who happens to be near the tank at that particular moment.

Examine Carefully

There are other important things to examine while you're inspecting the domestic hot water heater. Look for signs of corrosion at the connections of the incoming and outgoing water pipes at the top of the heater. Check the domestic hot water heater itself at the top and all around the sides for signs of corrosion. This corrosion is warning you that the unit may be nearing the end of, or has already ended, its life expectancy.

It's also necessary to check the vent at the top of this tank. This sheet metal vent line carries the gas fumes and the operating heat of this unit up into the chimney. If it is rusted, pitted, or damaged, carbon monoxide may be leaking into the house. See if any sections of this flue pipe have been taped, or if there are pieces of metal overlapping the existing metal flue pipe. These are indications that the flue pipe is damaged and that it is going to have to be replaced immediately. Look for black marks around the ignition controls of the gas-fired heater. These black marks are alerting you to the fact that there is a poor combustion mixture of gas and air. Usually this indicates that there is not enough air in the gas mixture at the time of combustion. A licensed plumber of the utility company will have to be called to adjust the heater for proper combustion to correct this problem.

An electrically fired domestic hot water heater has a heating element inserted into it near the bottom of the tank and the size of the tank determines how many heating elements have been inserted. Look at the identification plate at the bottom of the tank to find out its capacity and recovery rate as well as the amount of wattage used. The voltage requirement for this heater is 240 volts. Storage capacity in the tank can range from 30 to 140 gallons. The electric requirements, or wattage, depend upon the size of the tank and range from 1600 to 7000 watts.

Electrically fired domestic hot water heaters do not produce gas fumes; however, the problems associated with sediment in gas heaters also can occur in electric heaters. The iron and lime contents in the water produced by an electrically fired heater adhere to the heating element in the tank. As the sediment builds up, it reduces the life expectancy of the heating element in the tank. Check the incoming and outgoing water connections for corrosion as well as the tank itself for evidence of a corrosion problem. There also should be a pressure safety valve on this type of hot water heater. Electrically fired heaters usually have a five-year warranty from the manufacturer.

An oil-fired domestic hot water heater must be installed in accordance with the codes specified by the National Fire Protection Association as well as those set forth by local fire safety codes. The capacity and recovery rate can be found on the identification tag at the front, just as they are on the gas-fired heater. Again, a pressure safety valve should have been installed on it and an adequate draft is needed for proper combustion. Since the products of combustion in these types of heaters must be vented by a flue pipe up into the chimney, you should check the condition of the flue pipe for any damage and to be sure it is not blocked.

ELECTRICAL SERVICE

If you intend to purchase an older home, one of the problems you will often encounter is the need to upgrade the electrical system in that house. You'll probably find that the electrical system is a 110-volt system with anywhere from 30- to 60-ampere service housed in a fuse box instead of the circuit breaker panel box which is used in today's homes. This amount of electrical service is not adequate for today's standard of living.

Another way to estimate the capacity of the electrical service in a house is to count the number of outlets and switches installed around the house and to see whether or not there are any separate air-conditioning lines running through the house. Usually the total number of outlets and switches throughout a house with a low-capacity electrical system is small. It has been my experience to find only two or three outlets in the kitchen, two in the living room, one in the dining room, maybe one or two in each of the bedrooms, one in the main bathroom and none in the secondary bathroom or toilet facility. Usually there are no outlets outside, except perhaps one in the garage. Also, if the system is old, many of the outlets are not modern. Some houses that have not been updated at all use pull-chain lights instead of switching mechanisms to control lighting. Bear in mind that the wiring in a very old house probably is the original wiring, unless new panel boxes were installed and the house was then completely rewired. This old wiring could be a problem because it may already have become brittle and dry, and the insulation around it also may be dry.

Even if new panel boxes have been installed, be sure to ask the owner if the rest of the house was rewired, although usually this is not the case. Often in a house where a new panel box has been installed but the rest of the house has not been rewired, you will find that one circuit breaker is being used to service many circuits. If all of these circuits are put into operation at the same time, there will be a blowout and the breaker will have to be reset. Although many older houses have this kind of problem with the electrical system, it really is not a safe condition. To check for this problem during the inspection, turn on switches and other electrical appliances simultaneously and note if the lights flicker or if there is a blowout.

To modernize the electrical service, it will have to be updated to a 110/220-volt system with minimum 100-ampere service. A circuit breaker panel box (see illustration G) is going to have to be installed with a main shut-off breaker in the panel box to shut off the electricity in the house completely in case of an emergency. The circuit breaker panel box will have to be adequately sized so that circuit breakers can be added as needed. It also will be necessary to install separate outlets for the washing machine, dryer, refrigerator, and for each air conditioner. It would be a good idea also to change any pull-chain fixtures so that they operate on switching mechanisms and to install ground-fault interrupter type outlets in the kitchen and bathrooms as well as outside. In fact, depending upon the location of the house, the ground-fault interrupter type outlets may be required by the local electrical code. Additionally, if the house is very old, all new electrical circuitry will have to be run throughout the house and, at the same time, it may be a good idea to add ground-fault interrupter outlets in the garage.

One last but very important thing to be on the lookout for is if there is aluminum wiring in the existing electrical panel box or at a receptacle. This wiring should be replaced with copper wiring. Aluminum wiring is a potential fire hazard and it should be removed and replaced with copper (see Chapter Five for more information on aluminum wiring). In some localities, aluminum wiring is a violation of the local electrical code. Also, you may want to see if there is overhead or underground electrical service (see illustrations H and I). The only difference is that overhead electrical lines can be destroyed during heavy rainstorms and blizzards.

WATER MAIN

In many older homes, the existing water main either may still be the old lead main, or it may have been replaced with a copper main. It is important to determine if the existing main is made of lead or copper. Lead mains have many problems associated with them, not the least of which is that they can add lead to the contents of the drinking water. This is a serious health threat, especially in a house with children. Also, since the main is lead, it is old and can fail at any time. Today the cost of replacing a water main, depending upon the locality, can run as high as $2,500. It is this prohibitive cost that can make people wait for it to fail before they have it replaced.

While you're inspecting the water main, you also should be checking a variety of other things (see illustration J). First, be sure that the water shut-off valve is operating properly. If the existing main is lead, most likely the valve is as old as the main and it probably hasn't been opened or closed for many years. You can bet that it's not going to shut properly. It has been my experience to find that when I turn the shut-off valve handwheel, it just keeps right on turning. The valve simply does not function anymore. Even if the main is a newer type and it is not lead, you should inspect the shut-off valve to be sure that it functions properly. Also look to see if a drain valve has been installed after the water main valve. This drain valve is opened to drain the plumbing system thoroughly when work is going to be done on the plumbing system. The plumbing system also can be drained partially by opening the faucets at the various sinks, etc.

If the main valve doesn't operate properly and a drain valve has not been installed, plan on getting both installed if you buy the house. This may cost as much as $1,000, but these are important items. Even if the main valve and the drain valve are in place and are operating properly, but the main is lead, you should seriously consider having a copper main installed with a new main valve and a new drain valve. This can cost as much as $2,500, depending upon the house's location, but these are essential items and very worthwhile in the long run.

Other Items to Check

There are two other important things to look at while you're inspecting the water main. First, see if the electrical ground from the electric panel box is attached to it. If not, the ground should be attached immediately. The second thing is to look for the location of the house trap. Usually the water main runs into a pit that houses the main house trap (see illustration J). In many older houses, this house trap sits in a pit with soil around it. Check to see if the soil is wet around the trap. If it is wet, the house or main sewer line has to be cleaned. Sometimes there are roots growing into the sewer lines and these roots are causing water to back up into the house trap pit. In many older localities, the

storm and sanitary services are run together through a common house trap. During a heavy rainstorm, water coming off the roof, down through the gutters and leaders, and into the house sewer cannot drain to the main sewer because roots are blocking it. Instead, the rainwater backs up into the pit and into the cellar or basement. This is why it is wise for the homeowner to call a sewer cleaning service annually to have the roots removed from the sewer pipes. This precautionary measure can prevent flooding in the basement or cellar and the destruction of property stored there.

Also remember that if you see the soil is wet in the pit and you notice water stains around the pit floor, you could be looking at a major drainage problem with the main sewer line itself, instead of a problem with a blockage from tree roots. This kind of problem usually will cause excessive flooding in the basement or cellar.

PLUMBING

It's common to find an assortment of plumbing materials when inspecting an older house, especially in cases where some modernizing has been done. Galvanized piping, brass piping, and copper tubing used for water service can be found in a variety of combinations in these houses. Ideally red brass piping and copper tubing should be used for water service. A mixture of materials can indicate that a new bathroom facility has been installed, or that some of the existing plumbing failed, probably the galvanized piping, and it had to be replaced. Be prepared to face more plumbing failures, if you decide to purchase a house with this condition in it.

Galvanized Piping

Galvanized piping was commonly used during the 1930s for water service, but it has since been determined that it is not a suitable material for this use. Over a period of time, galvanized piping breaks down internally, the lines clog, and water pressure decreases as debris builds up in it. Also, as it ages, leaks develop at the threaded elbows, T's, and valves. If you find sections of galvanized piping in the house you're inspecting, you can anticipate that these sections are going to have to be replaced as they fail, if you purchase the house. To locate galvanized piping in a house, bring a magnet with you. If the magnet adheres to the piping, it is galvanized piping. (Remember that a magnet also adheres to black iron pipe which is in use for gas service.)

Another indication of the presence of galvanized piping in a house is brown, rust-colored water coming out of the faucets when you open them. This rust is sediment from the galvanized piping that is flowing through the plumbing. (Be aware of the fact that sediment can come out of brass piping too, but this only will occur when the water fixtures have not been flushed for an extended period of time, such as when a house has been left empty over the summer, or if the water line in the street has been repaired.)

Yellow Brass Piping

It is also common to find yellow brass piping in older houses. Yellow brass is an earlier form of brass piping and it differs from modern red brass in that it has a higher zinc and lead content. This combination is inferior to red brass because it can cause cracking and corrosion. The best way to identify yellow brass from its newer red form is to look for its yellow color. Yellow brass piping has a tendency to pit as it ages, causing leaks to occur. Older houses that have been modernized generally have a mixture of red brass piping and copper tubing in use to replace the yellow brass. Today's newest houses use copper tubing extensively. Some of them have vinyl and stainless steel flexible tubing in use to make connections under the sinks.

If you decide to purchase a house with galvanized and/or yellow brass piping in use, prepare yourself for future plumbing costs that are inevitably going to occur. I usually recommend that if you intend to make a major renovation after you buy the house (by that I mean new bathrooms and a new kitchen as part of the renovation project), then run all new red brass piping or copper tubing throughout the structure where plumbing is going to be required. On the other hand, if you intend to keep the old bathrooms and kitchen, get used to plumbing problems on a fairly regular basis. These will not necessarily be small problems either, since you may have to open walls to repair the riser piping that is running to an upstairs bathroom or kitchen. Old galvanized piping and yellow brass piping are going to be a constant nuisance because of the inevitable leaks and failures that will occur in the system at any time. It may be a better idea to look for a different house if you cannot or do not want to have to deal with these problems.

Bear in mind that even if you find wonderful new plumbing, leaks can still occur. Just bite the bullet, as they say, and have them fixed as soon as possible before the leaking water destroys something else and makes repairs even more expensive. Like heating, plumbing is one of the key systems in a house and it must be maintained properly and promptly to prevent unnecessary annoyances and expenses (see illustration K).

Drain Lines

The drain lines in a house, depending upon its age, are usually galvanized, cast-iron, or plastic. The waste lines from the water closets are either cast-iron or plastic. The main drain line running to the house sewer line is usually cast-iron. Generally parts of these lines are visible in an unfinished basement or cellar. If you can inspect them, look for leaks and signs of corrosion around fittings. If the house is old and sections of the galvanized or cast-iron lines have been replaced, they will have been replaced with plastic drain lines, or newer galvanized or cast-iron lines. This can indicate that either there was a problem with the drain lines, or that a plumbing renovation was done. In some localities, the plumbing code does not allow plastic lines to be used.

In many cases, there is one main drain line, usually 4″ in diameter, coming down from the upper floor bathroom. This vertical line takes the drainage from the upper floor bathroom and from the main level kitchen and bathroom or toilet facility. The line runs down to the basement or cellar where it connects into the house sewer line, which then drains into the town or city sewer system.

The section of line above the upper floor bathroom continues upward through the attic and out of the house through the roof. This section is called the vent stack. It functions as the vent for the plumbing system to clear it of sewer gases and to maintain atmospheric pressure in the drain lines. This prevents sewer gases from entering the house. If a vent stack is not installed in the house's plumbing system, it is a violation of the plumbing code. Sewer gases are dangerous and can even be deadly (see illustration K).

SUMMARY

Heating System

Types: Steam (oldest), Hot Water, Forced-Air (newest)
Fuels: Gas, Oil, Electric
Hot water produced in boiler, or in domestic hot water heater (see separate section on domestic hot water heater).
Central air conditioning operates with forced-air system.

Look to see if coal-fired boiler has been converted to gas- or oil-fired, generally large boiler with low efficiency rate. Check fire box in converted system for bricks which may be crumbling, loose, or broken. See if fire box needs to be cleaned. Look, don't touch, when cool.

Steam, Hot Water Systems: Look for water stains at base of boiler, water on floor, broken gauge glass, corrosion on outer cover of boiler.

Turn boiler on using wall thermostat. Throw shut-off switch attached to boiler to test, repeat with emergency shut-off switch to turn off boiler. Be sure pressure safety valve is on boiler.

Look for maintenance tag attached to boiler to see last date serviced, type of repairs done.

Leave boiler operating ten to fifteen minutes to be sure flue pipe exhausts properly and chimney is clear. Too much heat around boiler means gases not venting out chimney; shut off immediately, call for service.

Look for cracks or broken pieces of cement connecting flue pipe to chimney wall.

Oil-Fired System: See if oil-burner gun is old or new. Old one needs to be replaced.

Electric Forced-Air System: Be sure wiring meets local electrical code. See that furnace is centrally located in house. Heat pump used in heating also can be used to cool house.

Gas-Fired Forced-Air System: See if heat exchanger is cracked or broken, shut off immediately, call for service. Check that air flow across heat exchanger is uniform, flames are centered, flames heat bottom of heat exchanger.

Radiant Floor Heating: Copper or steel tubing means it is old system, water heated to 120–150 degrees in older systems, 80–100 degrees in newer system. Copper and steel tubing can develop leaks due to corrosion, or rupture in concrete slab. See if wood floor is buckled or warped; will be expensive to repair.

Domestic Hot Water Heater

Fuels: Gas, Oil, Electric
Coil in Boiler: Boiler must fire to heat water, puts strain on boiler, adds to fuel costs. Remove cover from boiler, look for water stains or rust where coil is inserted into boiler, means potential problem with coil.

Gas or Oil-Fired Heater: Ten years average life expectancy.

Look at front of tank for tag to get capacity in gallons and recovery rate in gallons-per-hour. Ask owner if unit was ever drained or flushed. Check for pressure safety valve and a pipe down side of unit ending near floor. Look for corrosion at incoming and outgoing water pipes at top of heater and all around heater itself.

Check sheet metal vent line at top of tank for rust, pitting, damage, patched sections, or taped sections showing aging. Look for black marks around ignition control of gas-fired heater.

Electric Hot Water Heater: Look at identification plate at bottom of tank for capacity, recovery rate and wattage, usually 240-volts, 1600-7000 watts. No fumes with this system, but sediment can adhere to heating element. Look for corrosion at incoming and outgoing water connections and on tank itself. Check for pressure safety valve.

Oil-Fired Heater: Look at identification plate at bottom for capacity and recovery rate. Check for pressure safety valve and for adequate draft. Check condition of flue pipe for damage, blockages.

Electrical Service

110-volt system with 30–60 amperes is old, inadequate. Count number of outlets and switches; too few means system is old, needs to be updated. Wiring probably old as well. In any case, ask owner if new wiring was ever installed.

See if one circuit breaker is servicing too many outlets, if so, lights put on simultaneously will flicker or blow out.

Look for 110/220-volt system with 100-ampere service minimum and circuit breaker panel box with main shut-off breaker in box.

Need to run separate outlets for washing machine, dryer, refrigerator, each air conditioner. Change pull-chain light fixtures to switches. Use ground-fault interrupter type outlets in kitchen, bathrooms, outside. Run all new electrical circuitry, if very old.

Beware of aluminum wiring, fire hazard. Replace with copper.

Water Main

Old lead main is health hazard, replace with copper.

Make sure water shut-off valve operates. See if drain valve was installed after water main valve. If not present, need to install both.

Be sure electrical ground is run to water main.

Look at pit which houses house trap to see if soil in it is wet. If wet, house and/or main sewer line must be cleaned. Tree roots could be causing blockage. Excessive flooding could be more serious problem with main sewer line.

Plumbing

Mixture of piping, such as galvanized, yellow brass, red brass, copper tubing, means there have been renovations and/or plumbing failures.

Use magnet to find galvanized piping; it will adhere to it. This is old piping, needs constant repair. Brown, rust-colored water coming out of faucets indicates presence of galvanized piping, if house has not been closed for months.

Yellow brass is older form of red brass. Can be seen by its color. Has tendency to pit as it ages, means plumbing failures, constant repairs.

When renovating bathrooms, kitchen, recommend change all plumbing to new to prevent failures which could be expensive. Even new plumbing sometimes leaks. Fix as soon as possible to prevent further damage.

Drain lines can be galvanized, cast-iron, or plastic. Check for leaks, corrosion, or for sections that have been replaced.

Check to see that vent stack pipe is installed. It should project above roof line.

2
Exterior

ROOFING

Ideally the best time to inspect a house is either during a rainfall, or right after one, in order to actually see how water-tight the house is. Naturally this is not always possible; however, there are other ways to obtain this information. For instance, look at the condition of the roof covering and of the gutters and leaders which carry the water off the roof and away from the property. Their condition can tell you if there already is any water leakage, or if there is a potential problem for water leakage into the house. Let me explain further.

When you examine the roof covering, take note of the slope, or pitch of the roof (see illustration L). A roof with a good pitch or slope is less likely to leak than a flat roof covered with roll roof covering. Another thing to look at is how the water is being directed off the roof. If the water is not being directed off the roof properly, the rainwater that collects or puddles on it can damage the roof. You should bring a pair of binoculars with you to view any intersections of the roof covering, that is, valleys where two sections of the sloped roofing meet. You also should examine the flashing around the chimney, or any other place on the roof such as around stack vents, to make sure it is intact. Also look for sections of the roof that have been patched because these patches can indicate poten-

tial trouble spots. Look for sections of different colored shingles. These can indicate that repairs have been done to problem areas.

The types of roof coverings used on most houses today include asphalt shingles, slate, wood (cedar) shingle, roll roofing paper, and terra cotta tile. The life expectancy of each of these coverings varies greatly, not only by type, but because of geographic location and environmental conditions in the area where the house is located. The roof covering manufacturers offer warranties for their products. Usually asphalt shingles last twenty years, a slate-covered roof could last thirty to forty years, and a more expensive type of slate can even last 100 years. Wood shingles, which are usually made of Western red cedar, last thirty-five to forty years. Roll roofing paper, depending upon its weight, can last up to ten years. Terra cotta tiles can last fifty to 100 years. All of these roof coverings are subjected to extreme temperatures, from horribly hot to bitterly cold weather conditions, as well as ice, snow, hail, etc., which can cause their life expectancy to be shortened dramatically.

Asphalt Shingles

When inspecting a roof covered with asphalt shingles, it's important to find out how many roof coverings are already on the roof. Ask the owner if the present roof covering is the second or third covering over the original. If the owner doesn't know, you can determine this for yourself by walking backwards away from the house about 20' to 30' so that you are standing far enough away from it to be able to see if the roof shingling tabs are lying flat on the roof. If you see a depression or a cupping effect (a wavy look) in the shingling material, this indicates that there is one or more roof coverings underneath, which is expanding and causing this effect. If there are two or more roof coverings, be aware of the fact that before a new roof covering can be installed on this roof, all of the existing roof coverings are going to have to be removed. A roof with more than two roof coverings can lead to water entry into the structure, and the damage it causes can be extensive and its repair, expensive.

While inspecting the asphalt shingles, if you see that the shingles are torn or that the coating of the shingling material is damaged, be aware that the roof is aging and that a new roof covering is going to have to be installed soon. Ask the owner how many years ago the present roof covering was installed, because the older it is, the more likely a new roof covering is going to be required shortly. While you're inspecting the roof covering, also look at the ridge of the roof. If the ridge is sagging, this could indicate that the ridge board is in need of repair. Then check the integrity of the ridge board when you're inside the house inspecting the attic.

Slate or Wood Shingles

When examining slate or wood shingles, look for damaged pieces of material. On a slate roof, look for pieces that are flaking, or that have white stains on them, which means that a new roof covering is going to have to be installed soon. If you see that the wood shingling material has broken, or is deteriorated, then this also is an indication that a new roof will have to be installed immediately. Ask the owner if the wood shingling is fire-treated. In some localities, local fire codes require that all wood

shingles be fire-treated. Remember that slate roof coverings are very heavy, much more so than asphalt or wood shingling. That's why it's important to inspect the roof structure to be sure that it is stronger for the slate-covered roof than it ordinarily would have to be for wood or asphalt shingle-covered roofs.

Rolled Asphalt Paper

The roof covering on a flat roof is rolled asphalt paper (see illustration M). The heaviest grade is the 90-lb. weight. Usually this type of covering lasts about ten years. Ordinarily you can climb up onto this flat roof via a ladder inside the house and walk around on it to see if the covering is eroding. Look for blisters (bubbles between the old and new coverings) which are signs of aging. In some cases, this means that blisters in the old roof covering were not broken before the new roof covering was applied. If the blisters are an indication of aging, usually the roof covering also shows signs of erosion. Also check the flashing around the skylights, stack vents, and the chimney to be certain that it is sound and that it effectively prevents water entry. Make sure that the hatch that you used to get onto the roof is sound and that when it closes, it seals tightly to prevent water entry and to block drafts from coming into the house. Look for eyelets and eye hooks on this hatch to be sure it locks securely. Make sure that the glass in the skylight is not damaged and that the TV antenna is not putting a hole into the roof covering.

Flat Roof

If the house you're inspecting has a flat roof, there may be a parapet wall around the perimeter of the roof. Usually the parapet wall is constructed of brick or stucco, and there are tile roof copings on top of the wall. In some cases, metal flashing is placed on top of the wall before the tile copings are installed. You may even see metal counter flashing at the base of the wall, which is overlapping the base flashing. The base flashing and the roof covering are made of felt (see illustration EE).

Check the condition of the wall first to see if it is cracked, or leaning inward or outward. Look for spalling or missing brickwork. Deteriorated brickwork and cracks are sources of water entry into the wall and eventually into the house. This water entry can undermine the wall structurally. Once the wall begins to lean dramatically, it is going to have to be rebuilt and this will be an expensive job. If it is not rebuilt, it may eventually fall down to the grade level below where it might seriously injure someone. This could result in a lawsuit, or worse.

If the parapet wall is stucco-constructed, again check its structural stability and look for areas of deterioration, as explained in the previous paragraph.

You should check the tile roof copings for cracks, broken sections, and loose copings. Also check the mortar between the joints of the copings to see if it is loose or missing. These conditions can cause water entry into the wall and house.

If the metal flashing and metal counter flashing have been installed, check to see if they are broken, missing, rusted, or rotted away. Again, these conditions are sources of water entry. Whether or not metal counter flashing has been installed, check the felt base flashing. This base flashing is applied to the base of the parapet wall and it overlaps the existing roof covering. Check this base flashing for cracks, blisters, or erosion. Sections that show these conditions are going to have to be replaced. They are other sources of water entry into the base of the wall and under the roof covering.

Finally, if the parapet wall has not been waterproofed, it is going to have to be waterproofed on the section that faces the roof covering. Do not use tar as a waterproofer because, over the years, it will dry and pull away from the brick parapet wall along with part of the brick facing. This condition may lead to open voids in the waterproofing which are sources of water entry.

If you happen to find a parapet wall that has already been tarred and you see the conditions described above, it can only be repaired by fixing the broken pieces in the wall and covering the entire wall with aluminum sheets to prevent water entry.

Terra Cotta Tile

When examining a terra cotta tile roof, look for missing sections of tile, for cracks, and for open pieces. These sections are going to have to be replaced immediately to prevent water entry and the damage that water will inevitably cause in the house.

GUTTERS AND LEADERS

While inspecting the roof covering on the house, also take a look at the gutters and leaders (see illustration L). On an older house, the gutters and leaders may be made of copper which might have tarnished to a greenish color. If they are discolored, they probably have already passed their life expectancy. You may find galvanized gutters and leaders on an older house instead of copper. Galvanized gutters and leaders show signs of aging when they are rusted and/or corroded. Usually these old galvanized gutters and leaders were painted only when the exterior was being painted. As a result of poor maintenance, there is a good chance that these gutters and leaders are going to have to be replaced shortly. If you see that some sections have already been replaced with newer sections of aluminum gutters and leaders, then the rest of the gutters and leaders are going to have to be replaced, too. Aluminum gutters and leaders are used today because they are much cheaper than copper.

In addition to the age and condition of the gutters and leaders, you should check the position and direction of the leader at the location where it comes down from the roof. See if it is connected to a drain pipe which runs into a drain line, or if it stops a foot above grade and allows water to drain out of this leader onto the soil. In the latter instance, if you decide to purchase this house, a section of pipe is going to have to be added onto the existing leader pipe. This will divert the rainwater run-off away from the foundation wall. If this is not done, heavy rainwater running down through the soil at the foundation wall can cause a seepage problem into the basement. Since there may already be a seepage problem there, look for signs of water entry in the basement at the same location as the bottom of the leader on the outside. If an additional piece of leader pipe cannot be added, then a splash block will have to be installed under the leader at the soil level to disperse the concentrated flow of water from the leader pipe. Another way to disperse this water would be to put a concrete slab under the area where the leader pipe drains and to pitch it away from the house. This slab should extend three to four feet away from the house when it is installed (see illustration N).

On the other hand, if the leader pipe is connected to a drain pipe which runs into the main sewer line, there are other potential problems to be aware of during the inspection. Over a period of time, leaves and other debris can lodge themselves at the elbow of the drain pipe which is below grade and this debris eventually will clog the drain pipe. Water will back up in it and, in some cases, will overflow the drain pipe at the grade level. The water will eventually work its way down to the foundation wall where it can cause a seepage problem. To inspect for evidence of this specific condition, check the back of the leader pipe to see if the seam has separated. If it has, the water that could not drain through it may have frozen in the leader pipe during the winter causing the seam to separate. This damaged leader pipe is going to have to be replaced and the drain pipe cleared so that it can function properly. Look for seepage near the location of the leader pipe/drain pipe while you're inspecting the basement or cellar for a sign of a clogged drain pipe.

In some cases, a clogged drain pipe can cause an even more severe problem and greater damage. The rainwater that cannot run through the drain pipe can actually back up in the leader pipe and up into the gutters. Water overflowing the gutters leaks into the wood fascia board behind them and, over a period of time, damages the fascia board. As

a matter of fact, if the condition is left unchecked, the fascia board will eventually rot and water will get into and damage the house. A simple way for the homeowner to prevent all of these expensive problems is to remove the leader pipe and clean the drain pipes annually so that rainwater can drain freely through them. A little regular maintenance can go a long way here.

EXTERIOR WALLS AND SIDING
Brick

When inspecting an exterior brick wall, you should look for a variety of conditions that can indicate problems exist. Examine the brickwork to see if it is cracked and whether or not the pointing of the brick is intact. Also check to see if there is a bulge in the wall. If the house is constructed of solid masonry and there is a bulge in it, it means that the mortar has failed. If the house is covered with a brick veneer, a bulge in it indicates that the metal ties used between the frame structure and the brick veneer have failed or deteriorated. Major masonry work will be required to repair the solid masonry wall as well as this brick veneer (see illustration FF).

Check the pointing of the brickwork to see if it is loose, crumbling, or wet. If the mortar falls as you inspect it, sections of the exterior brick wall are going to have to be repointed. Depending upon the type, cracks in the brick wall can either indicate that there's a problem with the foundation, or that there's a settlement problem. Be sure to inspect the brickwork over the windows. Usually the brickwork over a window or a door is supported by a steel lintel (see illustrations V and Z). In some cases, however, because of age and/or leaks into the brickwork, the lintel has begun to deflect. When inspecting for this condition, look for cracks in the vicinity of the brickwork which is being supported by the lintel.

Stucco

Many older homes have stucco exterior walls. Stucco is a mixture of Portland cement and sand.

After the tongue and groove sheathing was installed during construction of the house, wire mesh and roofing paper were installed over the sheathing. Then Portland cement and sand were mixed with water and troweled onto the exterior walls. The texture of this stucco generally was set by the person who applied it.

When you're examining stucco walls, look for cracks in the stucco because cracks can be a source of water entry. Also look for any bulges in the stucco wall. If you see a bulge, tap it lightly. If you hear a hollow sound, this sound indicates that the stucco has pulled away from the framing. If the bulge is small, it usually means that separation has occurred between the wire mesh and/or the sheathing. If the entire wall has bulged, however, especially near the center, it is an indication that the house's foundation may have had some differential settlement. Another possible cause for this bulge could be that the framing members to which the stucco, mesh, and sheathing were attached are undersized. In the latter instance, a costly renovation project is going to lie ahead if you decide to purchase this house.

Aluminum Siding

While inspecting the exterior of the house, ask the owner when the aluminum siding was installed. Run your hand over the siding in a number of places to see if the finish comes off onto your hand. The paint that comes off onto your hand may be a normal condition that is covered under the manufacturer's warranty. However, it also can be an indication that the siding is old and that it needs to be repainted. Look at the warranty to find out which is true in your particular case. Check the siding for dents, too. Aluminum siding dents easily when struck by hard objects, and these dents will be permanent unless the dented section of siding is removed and replaced. Find out if the siding was installed with a backup or insulation board behind it. If it was, the house is better insulated than if it has only been covered with the siding.

Since there's no way to look for yourself, ask the seller about the condition of the exterior material that is covered by the siding. Sometimes sidings are used to cover up cracked or deteriorating exterior walls. To approximate the age of the siding if the current owner doesn't know himself, look for vent holes along the bottom of each section of siding. Newer siding will have vent holes for its ventilation while old siding will not. Also after many years of exposure to the sun's rays, the color of the siding may be faded. Generally speaking, the newer the siding is, the longer it is going to last.

Vinyl Siding

The color of vinyl siding is homogeneous, that is, it has not been painted onto the siding material but actually is part of the siding. Vinyl siding has a greater resistance to dents; however, cold weather makes it very brittle and this can affect its ability to withstand a blow from a hard object. Again, if you see dents in vinyl siding, the dented section will have to be removed and replaced to make it look like new again.

Steel Siding

Steel siding can withstand being hit by a hard object better than aluminum or even vinyl siding. This siding, however, must have an electric ground since steel conducts electricity. This ground will keep the house grounded if lightning happens to strike it during an electrical storm.

Remember that no matter what kind of siding material you find being used on the house, be sure to check its condition carefully and to ascertain the condition of the exterior wall that the siding is covering. Feel the siding all around the structure to be sure that it is secured tightly to the exterior walls. Loose siding may indicate that the wall behind the siding is damaged, or that nails used to hold it on have come loose or fallen out. Also check to see if the siding is level. If it is not, this may indicate that there is a problem with the exterior wall under the siding, or that there is a settlement problem.

If the house you purchase doesn't already have siding on it, you may want to have it covered with siding yourself for easy maintenance and to add extra insulation. To decide what type of siding to use, look at the manufacturers' catalogs and carefully review their warranties and guarantees. It's especially important to take note of what they say about how long the color will last on the siding. Once you've picked the kind of siding you'd like, start looking for a contractor who is experienced in using this siding. Ask for recommendations and go to see samples of the contractor's work. Satisfied customers are the best way to judge a contractor's abilities and honesty.

Wood Siding

Many homes have what is called beveled clapboard siding on them. Usually this siding has been painted. First stand at each corner of the property to see if the siding is level along the exterior walls and to look for bulges that make it look wavy. Then check the siding for any damage. If you see that pieces are damaged or rotted, water may have gotten behind the siding, there may be insect infestation, or there may be a problem with the foundation of the house. This type of damage also can be revealing a problem with the sill plate at the bottom of the structure. All of the damaged siding will have to be replaced.

Make a careful inspection of the paint on this siding. If the paint was not applied properly, the siding is going to deteriorate, if it hasn't already done so. There are ways to detect whether the siding was painted properly. Paint could not adhere to the siding properly if the surface was not clean and dry when the paint was applied. The dirt, grease, or oil left on the siding caused the paint to dry too slowly. This condition is evident when the finish has an "alligatored" effect. Eventually the paint will flake and/or peel off of the siding. Blistered paint on the siding is caused by holes and cracks in the siding that were not filled and sealed properly before the paint was applied. Moisture was able to get behind the paint coating and this mois-

ture caused the paint to blister. Also paint that has been thinned down too much and then applied to the wood siding is not going to last very long. After it has dried, the paint will crack, blister, or even sag. In any case, the loose paint will have to be removed and new paint applied to prevent damage to the siding. Pieces that already are damaged will have to be removed and replaced before the painting is done.

Asphalt Shingle Siding

When you're inspecting asphalt shingle siding, look to see if the shingles are worn, damaged, or if they fall apart in your hands when you touch them. Check to see if the nails are secure. If you find any or all of these conditions, the house is going to need new shingles shortly. These conditions also mean that there are sources of water entry through the siding into the house. When new siding is installed, any other damage to the house is going to have to be repaired.

Asbestos Shingle Siding

If the asbestos shingle siding on the house you're inspecting has been painted, first look to see if the paint is flaking or peeling. If so, the siding is going to have to be repainted right away. Check to see if the nails which are holding the shingles in place are intact. Loose nail heads mean that the shingles are loose, too. See if any sections of shingling are cracked or broken. Since asbestos is a known carcinogen, these shingles will have to be removed by a certified asbestos removal company. Homeowners should not do this job themselves (see Chapter Five for more information on asbestos).

Redwood and Cedar Siding

In some areas of the country, redwood and cedar wood siding are the preferred siding materials. Unless a good grade of oil-based primer has been applied first, paint will not adhere properly to the cedar or redwood because of the resins in these woods. Left untreated, the wood will turn shades of gray, or weather, as the process is called, a condition usually preferred by those who choose these sidings. As untreated redwood weathers, some sections of the wood first turn black. Don't mistake this blackness for deterioration. In harsh climates, it is best to treat these sidings with a water-repellent preservative. If cedar siding is left unprotected, environmental conditions may damage it, particularly at the joints and fastening points.

WINDOWS AND DOORS

During the inspection, be sure to check the types and condition of the windows and doors. Also look at the condition of the storm windows, if they have been installed. While examining the outside, determine whether the existing windows are the house's original windows. Look to see if they need scraping, puttying, or painting. If the window sashes, jambs, or sills are rotted, they are going to have to be replaced. Sometimes storm windows have been installed over the original windows. It has been my experience that once storm windows were installed, owners had a tendency to forget to putty and paint the wood windows behind them. Look to see if they need to be painted.

Double-hung wood windows installed in older houses are able to lift up and down by means of sash cords or chains which are attached to window weights. These weights are housed behind the window jambs in hollow areas on each side of the window. If you notice that the existing windows are deteriorated, or for that matter even if they are in good condition, you may want to replace them if you purchase the house. You will want to remove the single-glazed wood windows that are not very energy efficient and replace them with double-glazed windows with what is called Low-E glass. This would greatly improve the house's energy efficiency. And since the window weights can now be removed, the hollow areas can be filled with insulation to enhance the house's energy efficiency (see illustration GG).

Window manufacturers and the types of windows that they produce are many and varied nowadays.

There are multiple glazings and coated glass as well as gas (Argon) fillings being offered by the manufacturers. Added layers of glass and glass coatings can save a large amount of heat that would ordinarily be lost through single-glazed double-hung windows. There are double- and triple-glazings available as well as Low-E glass in double-glazing.

Low-E coatings reflect the exterior heat away from the house, an important feature in the summer, but during the winter, these coatings keep the heat inside the house. Both coatings and glazings are available in sliding and French doors as well as in windows. Some manufacturers offer the glazings and coatings in a wood frame window; however, today it has become popular, especially from the point of view of maintenance, to buy these wood windows encased in either a vinyl or aluminum covering. Vinyl or aluminum-covered windows can be purchased in double-hung, casement, awning, or sliding windows, or in a combination of these types. Bay and bow windows also are available from the manufacturers and custom windows of all shapes and sizes often can be accommodated though usually not without additional cost. One of the best ways for the homeowner to decide what types of windows to use to replace existing windows is to review the manufacturers' catalogs. Compare the type of construction used in making the windows and the technical specifications, including the R value (which is the thermal resistance of a window) and the U value (the heat transfer coefficient of the window).

Another type of window the homeowner might want to consider is the direct replacement window, which is either an aluminum window with a thermal break, or a vinyl replacement window. These windows are installed directly into the window opening after the old wood sashes have been removed. Once again, in order to pick the type of window to use, the homeowner should review the manufacturers' catalogs and compare the R and U values of the various windows. It's not a good idea to use a simple aluminum replacement window because the heat inside the house is going to be lost by conduction through the cold exterior frame of these windows. You can actually see evidence of this heat loss where drops of condensation collect on the inside frame of the metal replacement window. The homeowner should at least consider using an aluminum window with a thermal break. This thermal break is important because it separates the interior and exterior sections of the aluminum frame and prevents heat loss by conduction through the frame.

If the house you're inspecting already has newer high-efficiency windows installed, you're looking at a more energy efficient house than it would otherwise be. However, if you see drops of condensation between the two panes of glass on a double-glazed window or door, this means that the seal around the double glass has failed, and a new double-glazed sash or door section is going to have to be purchased and installed.

Exterior Doors

While inspecting the outside of the house, check the condition of the exterior doors. If the doors are made of wood, see if they have been maintained properly. Examine the condition of the paint or stain. Check the door itself to see if it is cracked or damaged in any way. Try to open and close it. Check to see if it closes snugly against the door stops and if it locks securely. Look for any rot or deterioration at the base of the door and door jambs. Take note of how much space is left between the bottom of the door and the threshold. If there is an opening at the bottom of the door, a great deal of cold air can come in during the winter, and moisture also can enter the house.

After you've purchased a home, you may want to install a storm door in front of the wood exterior door. A storm door extends the life expectancy of the wood door by protecting it from severe weather conditions.

An exterior wood door with lots of glass in it, especially one that is single-glazed, is an energy problem, but it also may be a security problem. If the door is damaged or deteriorated, you are going to have to replace it and, perhaps, the door jambs also are going to have to be replaced, if they are in bad condition, too. I recommend that you have an energy-efficient exterior door installed with a deadbolt lock in it for security. As a matter of fact, some home insurance companies will give you a discount on the cost of your policy, if your exterior doors have deadbolt locks installed in them. Today there are many beautiful doors available — wood and steel — that are both energy-efficient and durable. Again, look at the manufacturers' catalogs to compare the construction of these doors and for explanations of their many special features.

SUMMARY

Roofing

Best time to inspect is after rainfall to check how watertight, but also can see by condition of roofing, gutters, and leaders.

Look for slope or pitch of roof, if rainwater puddles or collects on roof. Use binoculars to check valleys in sloped roofing. Check flashing around chimney and stack vents. Look for patched sections or different colored shingles to find repaired areas.

Types: Asphalt shingles, slate, wood (cedar) shingle, roll roofing paper, terra cotta tile. Life expectancy varies greatly by type used, geographic location, environmental conditions.

Asphalt shingles: Determine number of coverings by looking for depressions or cupping effect. More than two must be removed, if new covering needed. See if shingles are torn or if coating is damaged, which are signs of aging. If ridge of roof is sagging, ridge board needs repair. Look again when in attic.

Slate, wood shingles: Look for damaged pieces, missing sections. Slate may be flaked or have white stains if aging. Wood shingling broken or deteriorated needs to be replaced. Wood shingling must be fire-treated. Slate roofs very heavy so be sure structure can carry extra loading.

Rolled asphalt paper: Heaviest is 90-lb., usually lasts ten years. Can climb onto roof via ladder. Look for blisters or erosion for signs of aging. Check flashing around skylights, stack vents, and chimney for signs of water entry. Make sure hatch is sound, closes tightly, has eyelets and eye hooks for security. Check glass in skylight for breaks in it. See that TV antenna not putting hole in roofing.

House with flat roof may have parapet wall constructed of brick or stucco. See if wall is cracked or leaning. Look for spalling or missing brick; can lead to water entry and will undermine wall which will eventually fall to grade and cause injury.

Check tile roof copings for cracks, broken sections, loose pieces. See if mortar is missing or loose. See if metal flashing is broken, rusted, or missing. Check base flashing for cracks, blisters, or erosion. These all must be replaced to prevent water entry.

Waterproof parapet wall if not already done, but do not use tar. Tar will dry and destroy wall, opening sections to water entry. If wall is tarred, must cover with aluminum sheets to waterproof.

Terra cotta tiles: Look for missing sections, cracks, open pieces which invite water entry. All must be replaced.

Gutters and Leaders

Copper gutters and leaders may be discolored, greenish, if they are old. Galvanized gutters and leaders may be rusted or corroded if aging. Some old sections already replaced but will need to replace rest of old sections, or all, with aluminum gutters and leaders.

Check where leader comes down from roof, may run into drain line or stop a foot above grade. If stops above grade, will need to add section to divert water from foundation wall to prevent seepage. Also can use splash block or concrete slab to disperse water flow and pitch away from founda-

tion. When in basement, look for water entry in same location.

If leader pipe runs into drain line and then into main sewer line, leaves and debris may be blocking it. Water can eventually cause seepage problem in foundation wall. See if seam at back of leader is separated; if so, it must be replaced. While in basement, look for seepage in same location.

In some cases, water backup in leader pipe can damage gutter or fascia board. Look for rot or damage there. Water can even damage inside house. Homeowner should clean drain pipes annually.

Exterior Walls and Siding

Brick: Look for cracks and check if needs repointing. A solid masonry wall with bulge means mortar failed. A bulge in brick veneer means metal ties failed, must be replaced. Cracks in brick wall can mean foundation or settlement problem. Check lintel over doors and windows for deflection. Look for cracks in brickwork supported by lintel.

Stucco: Mixture of sand, Portland cement, and water applied with trowel over wire mesh and roofing paper on sheathing. Cracks in it are sources of water entry. Bulge that makes hollow sound when tapped means stucco pulling away from framing. Small bulge means separation behind stucco. Entire wall bulged means settlement in foundation or that framing members are undersized.

Aluminum siding: Ask owner age. Check if finish comes off onto hand and if covered by warranty. If not, siding needs repainting. Dented siding must be replaced. Ask if installed with insulation board or backup for better insulation of house. Ask condition of exterior walls under siding. Look for vent holes along bottom of siding to show it is relatively newer type of siding and newer installation. If color has faded, repainting needed soon.

Vinyl siding: Color is homogeneous. Greater resistance to dents but more brittle when cold. Dented pieces must be replaced.

Steel siding: Must have an electrical ground. Stronger than vinyl or aluminum.

No matter what kind of siding used, check condition carefully and determine condition of exterior wall underneath. Loose siding can mean wall underneath deteriorated or nails have fallen out. Siding that is not level can mean settlement problem or exterior wall deteriorated.

Siding is good choice for easy maintenance and extra insulation. Compare manufacturers' catalogs to pick one you like. Get experienced contractor to do work after checking recommendations.

Wood siding: See that siding is level, not wavy or bulging. Look for damaged or rotted pieces which are signs of water seepage, insect infestation, problem with foundation, or even problem with sill plate. Damaged siding must be replaced. Alligatored paint means surface was not clean and dry when applied. Blistered paint caused by holes or cracks improperly filled. Blisters also can mean paint was too thin. Old paint must be removed, damaged pieces replaced, siding repainted.

Asphalt shingle siding: Look for worn or damaged shingles. Loose nails may be because of water entry but new siding will be needed. See if paint flaked or peeled, if so, must repaint. Loose nails mean shingle loose, too. Look for cracked or broken pieces. Certified asbestos removal firm must remove them, not homeowner.

Redwood and cedar siding: Left untreated wood turns shades of gray, called weathering, usually preferred. Blackness on redwood not deteroiration but part of weathering. In harsh climates, treat wood with water-repellent preservative; cedar especially may be damaged if unprotected.

Windows and Doors

Check windows, doors, and storm windows to see if they need scraping, puttying, or painting. Rotted window sashes and/or jambs must be replaced. Original windows covered with storms usually not cared for properly.

Double-hung windows move up and down with weights behind window jambs. If deteriorated, or even if not, may want to remove and replace with double-glazed, Low-E glass windows to save energy. After weights removed, insulate hollow area behind jambs to increase energy efficiency.

Many window types include multiple glazings, coated glass, gas fillings. Available in doors, windows, sliding doors, French doors. Some wood windows available encased in vinyl or aluminum covering for easy care, such as double-hung, casement, awning, sliding, bay, bow, and custom-sizing. Compare manufacturers' catalogs including R and U values.

Direct replacement window also available in aluminum with a thermal break or vinyl. Again compare R and U values. Simple aluminum replacement window not good since heat lost by conduction through frame. This can be seen by drops of water on frames inside. Aluminum window with thermal break better to prevent heat loss by conduction.

House with high-efficiency windows and doors already is more energy efficient. Drops of condensation between two panes of glass mean seal failed and new sash must be installed.

Exterior Doors

Wood Doors: Examine condition of paint or stain. See if door is cracked or damaged. Open and close to see if it closes snugly and locks securely. Look for rot or deterioration at bottom of door and door jambs. Be sure cold air can't enter through space at bottom of door.

Storm doors: Extend life expectancy of exterior wood doors.

Exterior wood door with lots of glass may be security problem and energy problem. If door is damaged or deteriorated, check door jambs, too. Recommend energy-efficient exterior door with deadbolt lock. Compare manufacturers' catalogs to pick steel or wood door from among many beautiful choices.

3
Interior

FOUNDATION

When inspecting a house, one of the most important things to examine is the foundation. Depending upon the age of the property, the foundation may be rubble-constructed, concrete block, brick, or poured concrete. It may even be a mixture of the above, especially if an extension or some other addition has been built onto the house.

If the foundation walls are exposed in the basement or cellar, check the foundation walls for any bulges and/or cracks. The type of bulging or cracking that you see can indicate what type of potential problem lies ahead. Vertical cracks in the corner of a foundation wall may mean that the footing below the foundation wall has settled. If the wall is bulging inward, this can be an indication that the ground outside of the wall is exerting an inward pressure onto this wall. This inward pressure can be caused by water pressure, or it can indicate that repair work such as waterproofing was done on this section of the outside wall, and that the soil was not compacted properly against the wall after the work was completed.

Small cracks often can be found in the foundation walls in older houses. If they are not repaired, over a period of time, these small cracks can become sources of water entry. Cracks also can be found in new houses, usually right below the sill plate.

Generally these occur during the construction process when the foundation is curing. If not repaired, these small cracks also can become sources of water entry. In any case, an engineer should be called to evaluate the situation and to tell you exactly what is happening (see illustration HH).

Sometimes when you're looking at a foundation wall, you can see white deposits, or stains, on it. This condition is called "efflorescence." These deposits are salt deposits which are in the masonry and were brought to the surface. This condition is an indication of excessive dampness, and it means that the foundation walls are going to have to be waterproofed.

There are occasions when you cannot examine the foundation walls in the basement because they have been covered with paneling, Sheetrock®, or a similar type of wall covering. In this instance, you can still check the integrity of the foundation wall by taking a walk around the floors in the living areas. See if the floors sag, or if there is a noticeable settling in the house. As mentioned previously in the section on exterior walls, you should check the condition of the exterior walls. Also check to see if the doors and sliding doors close properly. Look at the jamb casings over these doors to see if they are level. When ascending or descending the staircases, check the skirt board of the staircase to see if it is pulling away from the wall (see illustration Y). Any of these conditions can be indications that there is a foundation problem. Again, if you have any doubts, call an engineer to inspect the foundation for you.

While you're inspecting the foundation, if you see that a large separation in the foundation wall has been repaired, don't panic. First ask the owner when this work was done. Ask to see the bill to determine what kind of guarantee the contractor gave to the owner for this foundation repair. It has been my experience that the guarantee on this kind of repair is usually good for five years. You must realize, however, that if you buy this piece of property, you have a problem with its foundation. This is another situation in which you might want to get an engineer's advice. Usually this type of condition in a foundation means that the foundation was poured on too hot a day, that the concrete mixture was weak, or that the soil on which the footing bears is not adequate for this amount of loading. It also can mean that the drainage of the soil around the foundation may be poor due to a high clay content in the soil. No matter which of these conditions has caused the foundation's problem, additional problems could lie ahead for the owner of this property.

FRAMING, JOISTS, AND ROOF RAFTERS

If you are inspecting a house built before the 1940s, it probably is a balloon-frame constructed house. Balloon-frame construction was developed in the 19th century. Shortly after the turn of the 20th century, this type of construction was modified to what is called platform-frame construction, and it is still used in today's home construction (see illustrations O and P).

A balloon-frame constructed house uses long 2 × 4 wall studs that are attached to the sill plate. The sill plate rests on the foundation wall. These 2 × 4 wall studs are run continuously up to the roof rafters. When this type of house was being built, local and national fire safety codes were not as stringent as they are today. Thus, a balloon-frame constructed house usually was not required to have horizontal fire-stopping built into the wall cavities. If a fire starts in the basement or cellar of this type of house, it can easily travel up through the walls to the upper floors and the attic (see illustrations O and Q).

In houses built using the platform-frame construction method, the joists are attached to the sill plate and the subfloor is laid on top of these joists. Then a 2 × 4 stud wall is constructed with a sole plate and a double top plate. These walls are only one story high. If the house is more than one story high, the framing procedure is repeated as often as there are stories in the house. In this way, each floor is separated by the double 2 × 4 top plates of the previous floor (see illustrations P and R).

While you're inspecting the basement or cellar, see if the joists are exposed. If they are, look to see if they sag, or if they're damaged. Look for additional joists that may have been sistered alongside of the original joists. In spots where new joists were sistered to the original joists, a section of the original joist might have been removed because of damage from insect infestation. Then take a walk around the floor above the basement or cellar to see if that floor is sagging or soft. A sagging or soft floor can indicate that the joists are undersized, or that instead of being spaced 16″ on center, they are spaced a greater distance apart from each other.

When inspecting a house that is more than 16′ wide, while you're in the basement, you can probably see that the wood joists supporting the first floor area above are not spanning the full width of the house. Most likely they are resting on an intermediate main beam, which is running perpendicular to the existing joists. Usually this beam is located in the middle of the cellar or basement and the wood joists are resting on it. Generally this beam runs the full length of the basement or cellar and its ends are embedded into the existing foundation wall. Depending upon the age of the house, the beam will be either a wood timber, usually 6″ × 6″ or 8″ × 8″, or a steel beam. This beam is supported by concrete-filled lally columns which rest on footings in the concrete floor slab.

There are a number of things to be aware of when inspecting a house of this size that has this condition in it. The lally columns, for example, should be made of steel and they should be concrete-filled (see illustration S). This is required by local fire safety codes in many areas. In some older houses that I've inspected, the columns being used to hold up the main beam were wood or even tree trunks. These types of columns are not fire-rated and, therefore, they are violations of most local building codes. In other houses that I've examined, whether new or old, although steel columns had been installed, they were not concrete-filled. Again, this is a building code violation. To be certain that steel lally columns are concrete-filled, hit the column with the handle of your screwdriver and listen to the sound that it makes. If you hear a hollow ringing sound, it is not concrete-filled. A dull thud generally means that it is concrete-filled. If lally columns are not being used, then concrete-filled steel lally columns should be installed.

When you're inspecting the main timber, look at both ends which are embedded into the foundation walls (see illustration S). It has been my experience, especially if the house is very old, to find that the ends of the timber are completely rotted, which means they are not resting solidly on the foundation walls. In other words, the foundation wall is no longer supporting the main timber. Also look for evidence of termite infestation at these ends, which could be compromising the support from the foundation wall. If you see either of these conditions, you will have to consider replacing the timber with a steel main beam if you decide to purchase this house. This work should only be done by an experienced contractor. The do-it-yourselfer may only cause more damage to the structure.

Another thing to take note of here is whether or not previous owners have removed any sections of the main timber, or even if they have moved one or more of them. Look for holes in the foundation

walls where the main timber used to be for evidence of this condition. Some of the lally columns also may have been removed, or moved, in order to have more open space in the cellar or basement. Check the spacing between the existing lally columns to see if lally columns have been removed or moved. Usually the space between them should be equal. If you find there is a great deal of space between two lally columns, then one is missing or has been moved to the right or left. When lally columns are removed, marks are left on the existing wood timber and/or on the concrete floor where the columns once were connected. If you find any of these conditions, call an engineer because the structure's support framing may have been compromised. Don't purchase this house unless an engineer says it is still structurally sound.

After you've examined the main timber, take a look at the joists which rest on the main timber and which support the floor area above. Look for a grade stamp on any of the joists (see illustration S). These joists should have either a No. 1 or No. 2 grade stamp, they should be kiln-dry, and they should be hem-fir, Douglas-fir, or another suitable species. If you see any joists with a No. 3 grade stamp, be aware that this is less suitable material for house framing and construction. Joists with a No. 3 grade stamp have a much lower allowable bending stress than those with a No. 1 or No. 2 grade stamp. Also, the distance these joists can span between supports is less than it would be for a No. 1 or No. 2 joist. Although I have not seen any houses yet with No. 3 floor joists, I recommend that if you happen to find one constructed with these joists, you consult with an engineer before making a decision about purchasing the property.

In some houses built around the turn of the century, as are many in the city where I live, you may be fortunate enough to find that longleaf heart pine has been used in the framing. This type of wood is no longer available in its new form because the trees were deforested from this country and can no longer grow here. Longleaf heart pine is only available as recycled flooring and paneling and as timbers. It is taken from old structures as they are being torn down and recycled for use. Longleaf heart pine is very strong and hard, which is why it was used in the 19th century for heavy construction such as shipbuilding and railroad bridge construction. Interestingly, the keel of the *U.S.S. CONSTITUTION* is made from longleaf heart pine. By the end of the 19th century, it was the major construction lumber used in housing construction, not only because of its strength, but also because of its excellent resistance to rot and insect infestation and its ready availability. So you can consider yourself lucky if the house you purchase has framing that is longleaf heart pine. You can't and won't find wood framing material better than that.

If the house you're inspecting is 16' wide or less, you'll probably see 2″ × 8″ or 2″ × 10″ joists, depending upon the species and grade stamp number, spanning the width of the house. Usually they are spaced 16″ on center. If the joists are spaced 12″ on center, then the house has been constructed better than one with 16″ on center spacing (see illustration JJ).

In the building construction process, the sill plate sits on the foundation wall. Wall studs and floor joists bear on this sill plate (see illustrations Q and R). That's why it is important to check the sill plate for rot and/or insect damage during an inspection. If rot or insect damage is found, the damaged section of sill plate is going to have to be replaced. This will be a job for a professional contractor, definitely not for the do-it-yourselfer.

As you walk around the floors, listen for any squeaks. These squeaks can indicate that a section of joists has deflected, that the subfloor is loose under the squeaky section, or even that there is no subfloor. If the floor slopes, this may be an indication that the house has settled over the years. As stated in the previous chapter on exterior walls, any indication that settlement has occurred could mean that there are problems with the framing members such as the joists, sill plate, etc.

While in the basement or cellar, look at the exposed floor joists for bracing, or solid blocking. Both are indications that the house is constructed solidly. When you look up at the joists, if you see that the subflooring is run diagonally, this is another indication that the house is well-constructed. Diagonal subflooring increases the house's bracing strength.

Go up into the attic and check the roof rafters. If they have not been covered with Sheetrock® or other drywall, it will be easy to inspect the roofing frame and the rafters for any damage. Look for signs of rot from water entry, or for any insect infestation. If any rafters have been damaged, they may require sistering, or if the damage is extensive, a section of the roof structure may have to be rebuilt. See if collar beams have been installed and, if so, check their condition for damage. Now is the time to check the ridge board, if you saw that the ridge board was sagging when you were examining the roof. See if the ridge board is cracked or deteriorated. Remember that the ridge board is the central point of stability for the roof rafters and if a section of it is damaged, a costly framing repair is going to have to be done by a contractor (see illustration T).

It's sometimes impossible to go up into the attic to view it because there is no subflooring to walk on. In this case, examine the attic from the ladder you're using to get to it. That flashlight with a powerful beam you brought will help you to see the attic. Take your time to examine it as best as possible, looking for all of the potential problems previously discussed.

While walking through the rooms below the attic level, look for water stains, or for badly damaged plaster ceilings and/or walls. Look for large cracks which may indicate that there are framing problems associated with the attic level below. Water stains may mean that there is water entry coming through the roof covering or the gutters. (See the following section for a complete discussion of this situation.)

INTERIOR ROOMS

Inspect each of the rooms in the house carefully. Check the plaster walls and ceilings for any damage. Large cracks or sagging plaster on the ceilings and/or walls may indicate that either the plaster is going to have to be covered with drywall, or that a major replastering job is going to have to be done. This condition also could mean that there are problems with the wall studs or ceiling joists. In a very old house, it's more than likely that a major plaster or drywall job is going to have to be done to repair the damage. Diagonal cracks around the window or door frames can mean that there's a problem in the wall framing, or even worse, that there's a settlement problem. If the house you're inspecting is fairly new and it is drywall constructed, you may see that some of the nail heads used to fasten the drywall are exposed, or that the tape used to join the drywall at the seams is exposed. In these cases, the drywall is going to have to be patched with joint compound wherever it is damaged or loose. Usually this condition doesn't indicate that there is a structural problem. It may look unsightly, but it can be resolved fairly easily.

Look at the ceiling for water stains. If water stains can be seen, there may be water entry through the roof, the gutters, or the exterior walls. Water stains also can indicate that there is a leak from either the kitchen or the bathroom on the floor above.

As mentioned previously in the framing section, you should walk around the floors listening for any squeaks, and feeling for sagging or softness in them. Any of these conditions can mean that there is a problem with the subflooring, or that the floor joists are not bridged properly.

Kitchen

When inspecting the kitchen, check the walls, floor, and ceiling for water stains and/or cracks. Look at the condition of the sink to see if it is cracked, chipped, or stained. Some local building codes consider a cracked or chipped sink a viola-tion and require that the sink be replaced. See if the cabinets are going to need to be refinished or re-painted, or if they're so badly damaged that they are going to have to be replaced. Make sure that the doors and drawers close properly. Look to see if the counter top is worn, burned, or stained. Check the water pressure and drainage by turning on the faucet at the sink. Fill the sink, let it drain, and listen for a gurgling sound, which may indicate that the sink is not vented (see bathroom section for more information on venting). As the sink drains, look for leaks at the trap underneath it. Check to see if there are shut-off valves on the hot and cold water lines under the sink. Count the number of electrical outlets in the kitchen. In many older houses, there are not enough outlets for today's food processors, coffee makers, microwave ovens, etc.

If the kitchen has not been modernized, but you want to purchase the house anyway, you are going to have to prepare for an expensive modernization project which will include new cabinets, counter top, and plumbing and electrical installations. Today's kitchen has become the focal point of the family, just as it was years ago, so a good modernization will be enjoyed for many years after its completion.

Bathroom

Check the walls, floor, and ceiling for cracks and stains. Inspect the condition of the bathroom fixtures, looking for cracks and chips. As stated previously, in some localities, cracked or chipped bathroom fixtures are violations of the building code. Look to see if the fixtures are the original ones, or if the bathroom has been modernized recently. Take hold of the water closet (toilet) and make sure that it is installed tightly onto the floor. Turn on the water in the sink, flush the water closet, and fill the bathtub to test the water pressure and drainage. After you have filled and flushed the bathroom fixtures, look for water stains on the floor and on the ceiling below this bathroom to see if there are any leaks coming from the bathroom fixtures. Flush the water closet again and look for water that might be coming out around the base. These leaks can indicate that the water closet flange, or the wax ring joint, is deteriorating and that a new connection is going to be needed.

While the sink is draining, look at the trap underneath it for leaks and to see that valves have been installed at the hot and cold water lines. Fill the sink with water, remove the drain plug, and listen for any gurgling sound as the water drains out of the sink. It's important to make this same test on each of the other fixtures. A gurgling sound is an indication that these fixtures have not been vented. Building codes require that all of these fixtures be vented, including all sinks as well as the washing machine. These vents are needed to clear the sewer gas out of the plumbing system. All of these vent pipes should project above the roof. Bathroom, kitchen, and laundry room plumbing can be connected to one or more vent pipes (see illustration K).

BASEMENT OR CELLAR

While inspecting the basement or cellar, look for any evidence of water seepage, or dampness, that might be coming in through the foundation walls. Also look around the floor for any noticeable water stains. If the walls are covered with paneling, examine the base of these panels, looking for any water stains. If the walls are covered with drywall, check the bottom of the drywall for damage, flaking, or water stains. If there is a musty smell in the basement, there could be a problem with high humidity in the basement or cellar. A cellar or basement needs a sufficient number of windows for proper ventilation. If humidity is high in the basement or cellar, a dehumidifier should be installed to lower the level of humidity there.

Water seepage into any basement or cellar is a severe problem because it can damage the house's foundation. The water must be prevented from coming into the basement immediately and the walls should be wire-brushed down and water-proofed to prevent further damage. One source of this seepage problem could be the gutters and leaders which were discussed fully in Chapter Two. As I said previously, if the gutters and leaders are the cause of the seepage problem, the water should be diverted away from the foundation by pouring concrete slabs along the foundation wall at the exterior grade level of the house. These slabs should be sloped away from the house and they should extend at least three feet from it.

Another way to solve this seepage problem, but one that requires a great deal of work and tremendous expense, is to dig down to the bottom of the foundation wall at the footing and then to waterproof the foundation wall completely again. A contractor will have to be hired to do this work, since the footing could be undermined as a result of the excavation.

In some areas, mostly low-lying areas or areas near large bodies of water, there may be a high water table which can cause water entry into a basement. The water actually enters from below the concrete floor slab of the basement. You definitely want to avoid this kind of problem. I recommend that you do not purchase a house that has this problem.

When examining the basement or cellar, inspect the pit that houses the house trap, as mentioned in the water main section in Chapter One. If you notice a number of water stains on the floor, they may have been caused when water backed up into the pit and overflowed onto the cellar or basement floor (see illustration J). Look to see if a sump pump has been installed in the pit. This sump pump is being used to pump water out of the cellar or basement. Water may be backing up into the basement because tree roots are blocking the sewer line, because there is a major leakage through the foundation walls, or even worse, because there is a major problem with the city, town, or county sewer main. If it turns out to be either of the latter two reasons, I recommend that you look for another house. These problems cannot be resolved quickly or easily and the damage to the house would be extensive.

Look to see if there is a crawl space in the basement or cellar. This crawl space usually has a dirt floor and is a couple of feet high. The floor joists supporting the living area above generally are exposed in this crawl space. If the crawl space is damp, either the soil in it is giving off moisture, or there is no ventilation in the crawl space. This moist vapor settles on the joists in the form of condensation, which is visible during the inspection. In order to restrict water vapor movement from the soil to the joists, a vapor barrier is going to have to be installed on top of this dirt floor. Look to see if a ventilator has been installed in the foundation wall near the top of the wall. Since ventilation is important in a crawl space, a ventilator is going to have to be installed, if you decide to purchase this house (see illustration KK).

ATTIC

When you inspect an unfinished attic, make sure that insulation has been installed in it. There may be a roll-type fiberglass insulation, or in an old house, a rock wool insulation, which is a loose-fill type of insulation, or there might even be vermiculite. Check to be sure that the plumbing vent line does not terminate in the attic. It should extend through the roof to the outside. If there are two or three layers of insulation, check to see that there are no vapor barriers on the layers above the one nearest to the living area. There should be only one vapor barrier in the attic and that one should be attached to the first layer of insulation nearest to the living area. If the additional layers of insulation have vapor barriers on them, these vapor barriers are trapping moisture coming up into the attic from the living area. This collection of moisture can eventually damage the wood joists in the attic. It will be easy to remove the additional vapor barriers by just picking up the existing layers of insulation and pulling the vapor barriers off each layer. Anywhere from 6″ to 12″ of insulation is a good amount to have in the attic. The amount of insulation needed depends upon the weather conditions in the area.

While you're in the attic, look to see if the attic is vented. Check to see if a vent has been installed. If not, moisture will build up in the attic during the changing seasons and the heating season, and it will damage the roof's framing members. If there is no ventilation in the attic, a vent window, a louvered vent, or a roof vent is going to have to be installed.

If the attic you're inspecting is being used as a living space, yet another problem could be found in it. When the attic was renovated into a living area, the roof rafters probably were covered with drywall. Also knee walls were constructed and these were covered with drywall to form the living area. The space that remained between the roof sheathing and the drywall was insulated and became a dead air space. Moisture builds up in this dead air space during seasonal temperature changes and the heating season and, over a period of time, damages the framing members of the roof. If you purchase a house with an attic that is being used as a living space, you should consider venting the dead air space between the roof sheathing and the drywall, if you see that this has not already been done. In order to do this, a ridge vent is going to have to be installed along the length of the ridge board and vented soffits will be required to provide for a natural flow of fresh air from the soffits to the ridge vent (see illustration U). When you check for insulation, be sure that it has not been pushed into the intersection where the roof rafters meet the ceiling joists at the soffit area. You may be able to check for this condition if there is a small doorway which opens into a narrow space behind the knee walls revealing the intersection of the roof rafters and ceiling joists at the soffit area. Air has to circulate in the air space moving from the vented soffits to the ridge vent and the insulation must not block the soffits and interfere with this air flow.

If you're inspecting a house with a flat roof, usually there is a space between the top floor ceiling and the roof covering called a cock loft. Generally this space is between 18″ and 24″ deep. If you do not see roof vents, they are going to have to be installed for the reasons stated above as well as to reduce the amount of heat that collects in this space during the summer months. This heat makes the living area below the cock loft very warm during the summer and it increases air conditioning costs because it is harder to cool that living space.

SUMMARY

Foundation is one of the most important things to examine. It may be rubble-constructed, concrete block, brick, or poured concrete, or even mixture of above, especially if addition built onto house.

Look for bulges or cracks in exposed foundation walls in basement. Vertical cracks in corner of foundation wall mean footing has settled. Wall bulging inward either from inward pressure on wall from ground outside, or improper compacting of soil against wall.

Small cracks often found in old foundation walls can be sources of water entry if not repaired. Cracks in new foundation walls, usually below sill plate, occur as foundation cures during construction. Also can be sources of water entry. All cracks should be examined by an engineer.

White deposits or stains, called "efflorescence," are salt deposits in the masonry which came to surface. Indicates excessive dampness and means foundation walls need waterproofing.

When foundation walls inside are covered with paneling or drywall, check integrity of foundation walls by walking around floor above. See if floor sags, or if house has settled. Look at condition of exterior walls. See if doors and sliding doors close properly. See if jamb casings over doors are level. Check skirt board of staircase to see if it is pulling away from wall. All are signs of foundation problems. Call engineer, if you have doubts.

If large separation in foundation wall already has been repaired, see bill to determine when work done and if work guaranteed. This condition means foundation problem exists. Engineer could examine for you. Foundation may have been poured on very hot day, concrete mixture may

have been weak, or soil under footings not adequate for loading. Also can mean poor drainage due to high clay content in soil around foundation. Any of these conditions means problems could lie ahead.

Framing, Joists, and Roof Rafters

Balloon-frame construction: Built before 1940s. Wall studs attached to sill plate, sill plate rests on foundation walls, wall studs run continuously up to roof rafters. No horizontal fire-stopping built into wall cavities, fire can easily travel up through walls.

Platform-frame construction: Joists attached to sill plate, subfloor laid on top of joists, one-story-high stud wall constructed with sole plate and double top plate. Framing repeated for each story so each floor separated by double top plate.

While inspecting basement, see if joists sag or are damaged. Look for joists sistered to original joists. Insect damage may be reason joists sistered. Walk around floor above basement to see if it sags or is soft. If so, joists may be undersized or spaced more than 16″ on center.

In house more than 16′ wide, wood joists rest on intermediate main beam in middle of basement. Beam runs full length of basement and ends are embedded in foundation walls. May be wood or steel, supported by concrete-filled lally columns which rest on footings in concrete floor slab.

Make sure lally columns are steel, not wood which is not fire-rated. Be sure lally columns are concrete-filled, listen for dull thud when hit by screwdriver. Hollow ringing sound means not concrete-filled.

To inspect main timber, look at both ends for rot, which means it no longer rests on foundation walls. Look at ends for termite infestation. If rotted or insect-infested, must install new steel main beam.

Be sure main timber was not removed, look for holes where ends were embedded in foundation walls. See that lally columns were not moved or removed by measuring space between them (should be equal), or by noting marks left on wood timber or on floor slab. If you find any of these conditions, call engineer to determine if support framing has been compromised. House may be structurally unsound.

Look at grade stamp on joists for No. 1 or No. 2 grade, kiln-dry, hem-fir, Douglas-fir, or other suitable species. No. 3 grade limited in bending stress and span. If found, consult engineer.

Houses built around turn of the century may have longleaf heart pine used in framing. Only available recycled now. Used in heavy construction because of strength and resistance to rot and insects. House framed with it is well-built.

In house less than 16′ wide, joists should be 16″ on center, 2″ × 8″ or 2″ × 10″. If joists 12″ on center, house is better constructed.

Check sill plate for rot or insect damage. Damaged section must be replaced by professional, not homeowner.

Squeaky floors can mean joist section has deflected, subfloor is loose, or there's no subfloor. Sloping floors mean house has settled which could mean problems with framing members.

Bracing or solid blocking in floor joists mean house built solidly. Diagonal subflooring also increases house's bracing strength.

In attic, check roof rafters for rot from water entry or insect infestation. Damaged rafters must be sistered, or if damage extensive, roof structure must be rebuilt. If collar beams are in place, check their condition. See if ridge board is sagging, cracked, or deteriorated. If a section is damaged, needs costly framing repair.

If attic without subflooring to walk on, examine from ladder with flashlight. Take time to see potential problems.

In rooms below attic, look for water stains or damaged plaster. Large cracks can mean framing problems in attic. Water stains may be from old roof covering or damaged gutters.

Interior Rooms

Check plaster walls and ceilings for damage. Large cracks need to be covered with drywall or new plaster and could indicate problems with wall studs or ceiling joists. Diagonal cracks around window or door frames mean problems with wall framing or settlement problem. In newer Sheetrock® construction, loose nail heads or tape need patching with joint compound. Usually not structural problem.

Water stains on ceilings may be from roof, gutters, exterior walls, or even from kitchen or bathrooms above.

Walk around floors to hear squeaks, or feel for sagging or softness, may mean problem with subfloor, or that floor joists not bridged properly.

Kitchen: Check walls, floor, ceiling for cracks or water stains. Check sink for cracks, chips, or stains. See if cabinets need refinishing, repainting, or replacement. Make sure doors and drawers close properly. Check counter top for wear, burns, stains. Check water pressure and drainage at sink. Gurgling sound when sink drains means sink not vented. Look for leaks at trap and for shut-off valves on hot and cold water lines under sink. Count electrical outlets. Modernization will be costly, but can be worthwhile.

Bathroom: Check walls, floor, ceiling for cracks or stains. Check fixtures for cracks and chips. Make sure water closet installed tightly. Check water pressure and drainage on all fixtures. Look for water stains on floor and ceiling below this room. Look for leaks around base of water closet and at trap under sink, and for shut-off valves on hot and cold water lines. Gurgling sound as water drains from any fixture means not vented. Vents clear sewer gases, should project above roof line.

Basement or Cellar

Look for water seepage or dampness coming through foundation walls. Look for water stains on floor. Check base of paneling for water stains, or bottom of drywall for damage, flaking, or water stains. A musty smell means there is high humidity in cellar due to poor ventilation. A dehumidifier must be installed.

Water seepage in basement is serious problem. Walls should be wire-brushed down and water-proofed to prevent further damage. If gutters and leaders are source of seepage, divert water away from foundation at exterior grade level with concrete slab that slopes away from house.

High water table in some areas causes water entry into basement. Water coming from below floor slab. Condition cannot be corrected, so look for another house in different area.

In cellar or basement, inspect pit housing house trap. Water stains on floor may be from water backing up in pit and overflowing onto floor. Look for sump pump being used to pump water out of basement. Water may be from tree roots blocking sewer line, major leakage through foundation walls, or major problem with town or city sewer line. If latter two, don't purchase house; if first, call root removal company.

Crawl space in cellar has dirt floor, is about 2′ high. If damp, moisture may be from soil or poor ventilation. Condensation on exposed floor joists in crawl space is evidence of dampness. Put vapor barrier on soil to restrict moisture's movement and install ventilator near top of wall.

Attic

Make sure unfinished attic has insulation, roll-type fiberglass, or in older houses, rock wool or even vermiculite. See that plumbing vent line doesn't end in attic. Be sure there is only one vapor barrier in attic and it is attached to first layer of insulation nearest to living area. Additional vapor barriers trap moisture, must be removed. 6″–12″ of insulation good amount in attic. Make sure attic is vented with window, louvered vent, or roof vent.

If attic is used as living space, be sure dead air space between roof sheathing and drywall is vented. Need ridge vent and vented soffits installed for proper ventilation. Be sure insulation not blocking air flow from vented soffits to ridge vent.

In house with flat roof, there is cock loft, space between top floor ceiling and roof covering, usually 18″ to 24″ deep. Be sure roof vents are installed to prevent moisture and heat buildup which increases air conditioning costs during summer months.

4
Extra Features

PATIO

The patio usually is constructed with patio blocks which are set down on a bed of sand. First the ground is leveled and compacted. Then a treated plastic liner is laid on top of the ground. This liner can be purchased from most garden supply stores. In addition to being chemically treated, it has tiny holes in it which allow rainwater to drain through it into the ground. The chemicals in the plastic liner as well as its tiny holes prevent vegetation from growing under and around the patio blocks.

The procedure for laying patio blocks is a fairly simple one. A bed of sand, usually about 2″ deep, is put on the plastic liner. This sand is leveled and compacted and the patio blocks are placed on top of it. After the blocks are laid in place, the joints between them are filled with sand. As the blocks settle further into the sand, especially after a heavy rainfall, some of the joints have to be refilled. A broom is used to push the sand into the joints. The perimeter around the patio blocks has to be enclosed in order to prevent the sand from running out from under and around the joints of the patio blocks. Today there are many styles and colors of patio blocks and they can make a very attractive patio when patterned carefully.

DECK

Decks should be constructed with redwood, Western red cedar, or pressure-treated lumber. Other wood products simply cannot withstand the weather conditions that a deck is subjected to such as rain, snow, heat, etc. Redwood and cedar are more expensive woods than pressure-treated lumber. Both redwood and cedar can be left to weather naturally, although in harsh climates, it is recommended that cedar be treated with a preservative to minimize cracking. If you want to achieve the weathered-look more quickly than nature can provide, you should coat the cedar or redwood with a bleaching oil. Never paint redwood or cedar without first applying a coat of a good oil-based primer, because the resins in these woods will cause the paint to blister and peel without a base primer coat. A good grade of galvanized or stainless steel nails should be used in the deck's construction. Other nailing products will rust and look unsightly.

If the deck is being built over an area with soil in it, you should be sure to prevent any growth of vegetation under it. The grass, weeds, etc., will collect moisture and encourage insect infestation which could damage the house as well as the deck.

To prevent any growth of vegetation, either cover the area with concrete, or use the plastic liner discussed in the paragraphs above about patios. If you're going to use the plastic liner in this application, instead of placing patio blocks on the plastic liner, put limestones on it. They will hold the liner down firmly and look attractive as well.

The preservative used in pressure-treated lumber usually is chromated copper arsenate and it is stamped on the lumber as "CCA" along with the grade stamp. This preservative is forced into the wood. Some of today's manufacturers of pressure-treated lumber guarantee it for life.

One of the things to remember about pressure-treated lumber is that usually it is kiln-dried before it is treated, so when the homeowner buys it, the wood has a high moisture content. As the wood dries, it has a tendency to warp, so the homeowner should use the lumber as soon as possible after it is purchased. Also, stack and bind your supply until you use it, and while you're using it, to prevent it from warping as much as possible.

POOL

An in-ground pool may be made of tile, concrete, or gunite. Ask the owner if a permit was issued for its installation. In many localities, a permit must be obtained before an in-ground pool can be constructed. The local building code requires that overhead power lines not be located in the area of the pool and that exterior outlets around the pool area be the ground-fault interrupter type. Lights and walkways also are required around the pool and some local codes even demand that the pool be surrounded by a fence and that signs be posted listing the various depths of the water in the pool. These are just some of the many regulations associated with in-ground pools. They are necessary to save lives, mostly the lives of children. In addition, since liability is severe in these cases, local codes should be adhered to strictly.

The plumbing for the pool's pump and filtering equipment always should be installed by a licensed

plumber, and the power requirements should be handled by a licensed electrician to be sure that local requirements are fully met.

If you learn that the in-ground pool is an illegal installation, that is, no permit was issued for its construction, then the pool is a violation of the local building code. As a result, you may not be able to get the mortgage from the bank until the pool has been removed. Depending upon its size and type of construction, this removal could be very costly.

GREENHOUSE/SUNROOM

Today there are many manufacturers of greenhouses offering a wide variety of styles and sizes to please everyone's tastes. In many areas, the local building code dictates that a building permit has to be issued before a greenhouse can be constructed. There are many glazing materials available such as glass, fiberglass, and acrylics. Depending upon the glazing chosen, the light coming through it may be direct or diffused. Diffused lighting is preferred for privacy; however, many plants need direct lighting for healthy growth. How you plan to use the greenhouse and what types of plants you want to grow in it will dictate what glazing you eventually choose.

The structural framing surrounding the glazing material can be aluminum or even redwood. If you intend to use it as a greenhouse rather than as a sunroom, you are going to need plumbing, heating, and ventilation as well as a floor drain for water drainage. Also a concrete slab will be needed for construction of this greenhouse, since the foundation has to be able to support a great deal of weight.

EXTERIOR GARAGE

Carefully inspect the condition of the structure, which is generally block, brick, or stucco-constructed. Look for any large cracks running through the structure. These large cracks can indicate that there is a settlement problem. Examine the construction of the concrete floor slab. If it is badly cracked or deteriorated, a new floor slab is going to have to be poured. Any large cracks in the exterior walls will have to be repaired to prevent water from entering through them.

While inside the garage, look up at the roof rafters to see if they are rotted or damaged. This condition could indicate that water is entering through the roof covering. While examining the outside, check the condition of the garage's roof covering. Often the garage roof is not recovered as often as the one on the house.

Check the condition of the garage door to see if the paint is peeling or the metal is rusted. If it is a roll-up type door, be sure that it rolls freely. Also examine the base of the wood jambs around the door to see if they are rotted. This deterioration may be caused by termites or dampness and the wood will have to be replaced.

INTERIOR GARAGE

Many of today's newer houses have been built with interior garages. These garages should be constructed with fire-rated materials. Usually a door has been installed at the rear or side of the garage and it opens into the living area of the house. This door also must be fire-rated. Just as you would do with an exterior garage, examine the condition of the garage door and door jambs to be sure they function properly, are secured tightly, and are not rusted, rotted, or damaged by insects.

If you purchase a house with an interior garage, never warm up your car in the garage during the winter. The fumes from your car engine's exhaust, which are carbon monoxide, could circulate into the living area of your house. Carbon monoxide is a deadly gas and it should be kept out of your house.

Whether your garage is the interior or the exterior type, if it has an electronically operated garage door opener installed, make sure that it is operating properly. It should stop as it is lowering when it hits any obstacle and go back up away from the obstacle. This is an important safety feature, especially for children and pets, since the door is heavy and could hurt them if it doesn't stop.

If the house you're thinking of purchasing has a wood constructed garage, I recommend that you look for a different house. Wood is highly flammable, therefore, it is not a suitable material for a garage in which you're going to store your car. Actually, in some localities, a wood-constructed garage is considered to be a fire hazard, and it is a violation of the local fire safety code. I've usually found that a bank will not grant a mortgage until this wood structure has been removed. In addition, it may be difficult to purchase home fire insurance if there is a wood-constructed garage associated with your house's property.

LANDSCAPING

Look at the condition of the landscaping while you're inspecting the outside of a house. Large tree branches that overhang onto the roof of the house or garage could be damaging the roof covering. After a heavy rainfall, the roof section that is covered by these branches takes a longer time to dry than the rest of the roof and this water will eventually damage that roof section. Also, these branches can work their way under the roofing material causing damage to it.

Large trees or shrubs that are planted close to the foundation also can cause damage. They can even open a path through the soil, which would allow rainwater to seep into the foundation. Dead trees and shrubs have been known to be good places to find termite infestation which is why they should be removed immediately. Once dead trees or shrubs have become infested with termites, they should not be burned in your fireplace. If you find termites in dead trees or shrubs in the garden, it's probably a good idea to call a termite exterminating firm to treat the house and garage which also may have become infested with them.

DRIVEWAY, STREETWALK, WALKWAYS, AND FRONT ENTRANCE STEPS

As you inspect a house, take note of the condition of the front entrance steps, the streetwalk, walkways, and the driveway. Look for a variety of possible problems that could lead to expensive repairs.

Driveway

If the driveway is made of concrete, check the condition of the concrete for cracks or erosion. If it is badly cracked or eroded, some sections may have to be repaired, but if it is badly deteriorated, the whole driveway is going to have to be replaced. Depending upon its size, this replacement could cost thousands of dollars.

If the driveway is covered with blacktop and it is only slightly cracked, it can be repaired easily by the homeowner. Patching material is available in hardware stores for quick, inexpensive repairs of this type. To keep the blacktop in good condition, it should be coated annually with a sealer which can be purchased from most hardware stores. However, if the blacktop is too badly damaged, a new driveway is going to have to be made. Again, depending upon its size, this can be a costly project for the homeowner.

Streetwalk and Walkways

Check the streetwalk and walkways for cracks and erosion. Sometimes a section of concrete streetwalk is damaged where the tree roots have lifted it up and cracked it. This section of the streetwalk should be repaired immediately since it is a tripping hazard, not to mention a possible lawsuit if someone falls and is hurt. A streetwalk that is badly cracked and/or deteriorated, whether from tree roots, aging, or any other cause, is going to have to be replaced. Again, its size determines how costly the project will be for the homeowner.

Front Entrance Steps

Carefully inspect the front entrance steps, which generally are brick, or concrete and brick-constructed. Examine the condition of the bricks, concrete steps, and sidewalls to see if the concrete is cracked, or if the bricks are cracked, spalling, or missing (see illustration V). If the steps are badly deteriorated, repairing or replacing them is going to be expensive. See if the sidewalls that run up along the steps are straight. If they are leaning out of plumb, another costly replacement project is going to have to be anticipated. If an iron handrail is attached to these steps, grab it to be sure it is anchored firmly. Look to see if the paint is peeling, or if the metal has rusted because of missing paint. If the house you purchase doesn't have a handrail attached to the front entrance steps, you may want to consider adding one for easier access up and down the steps, especially for the elderly and disabled.

CENTRAL AIR CONDITIONING

The central air conditioning system is used to cool a number of rooms and spaces simultaneously. The advantage of having a forced-air heating system is that this system's ducting also can be used to air condition the house during the summer months. In many houses, the air conditioning unit consists of a compressor, condenser coil, and an evaporator coil. Freon® is used as a refrigerant. The evaporator coil is installed in the duct work of the heating system above the furnace. Refrigerant piping is connected from the evaporator coil to the condenser coil and on to the compressor, which is located outside of the house. The air conditioning unit usually sits on a concrete pad. The name plate attached to the unit provides information regarding its capacity, power rating, etc. (see illustration D).

When inspecting the air conditioner, look for an electric panel box with a disconnect switch that should be near the air conditioning unit. The name plate on the unit indicates the amperage required and the type of box that should be used. The box with the disconnect switch attached to it must conform to what is stated on the name plate of the air conditioning unit. If it does not, it is a violation of the electrical code. For example, if the name plate on the air conditioner calls for a 50-ampere fused electric box with the disconnect switch, then that box must be a 50-ampere fused electric box, not a 50-ampere circuit breaker box (see illustration LL).

Usually an air conditioning unit has a five- to seven-year warranty. The unit should have been covered during the winter months to help extend its life expectancy. If you're inspecting the house during the summer, put the air conditioning unit into operation for an extended period of time to see how long it takes to cool the house. It should take about five minutes to feel the cooling effects of the air conditioning system.

SUMMARY

Patio

Patio blocks usually set on bed of sand after ground is leveled, compacted, and covered with treated plastic liner. Liner prevents vegetation growth which can displace blocks. Sand is used to fill joints between blocks. Many styles, colors available to create pretty patterns.

Decks

Should be constructed of redwood, Western red cedar, or pressure-treated lumber. Redwood and cedar can be left to weather, but in harsh climates, untreated cedar will crack. Bleaching oil on redwood or cedar gives weathered look more quickly. Never paint either one without first applying a coat of oil-based primer because resins in wood can cause paint to blister and peel if not primed. Use galvanized or stainless steel nails in construction. If deck has soil under it, cover with plastic liner and limestones to prevent vegetation growth, dampness, and insect infestation.

Chromated copper arsenate (CCA) used as pre-servative for pressure-treated lumber. Look for its stamp on wood. Wood has high moisture content which causes it to warp, so use quickly after purchasing.

Pool

In-ground pool may be made of tile, concrete, or gunite. Be sure installation done with permits. Building code may require no overhead power lines, only ground-fault interrupter outlets in area of pool, lights and walkways around pool, fence surrounding pool, and sign listing depths of water in pool. Liability is severe.

Plumbing for pump and filter must be installed by licensed plumber and power requirements by licensed electrician to meet local codes.

If pool installation is illegal, is violation of code and may have to be removed to obtain mortgage.

Greenhouse/Sunroom

Many styles and sizes available. Building permit usually must be issued. Many glazing materials such as glass, fiberglass, and acrylics for direct or diffused light. Diffused light preferred for privacy but most plants need direct light. Decision based on how it will be used.

Structural framing either aluminum or redwood. If used for plants, need plumbing, heating, ventilation, floor drain. Concrete slab needed to support weight.

Exterior Garage

Structure is block, brick, or stucco-constructed. Large cracks through structure mean settlement problem. Badly cracked and deteriorated floor slab needs replacement. Large cracks in exterior wall should be repaired to prevent water entry.

Inside garage look at roof rafters for rot or damage. Check roof covering outside for leaks and general condition. See if paint is peeling on door, or if metal is rusted. Be sure door rolls freely.

Check base of wood jambs around door for rot or insect infestation. If rotted or damaged, must be replaced.

Interior Garage

Should be made with fire-rated materials. Door leading into living area should also be fire-rated. Check condition of door and door jambs as above.

Never warm up car in garage during winter months. Fumes from exhaust are deadly carbon monoxide.

Whether interior or exterior garage, if garage door has electronically operated opener, be sure it stops descending when it hits obstacle to protect children and pets.

Don't purchase house with wood-constructed garage because it is very flammable and may be violation of local fire safety code. Usually bank will not grant mortgage until wood garage is removed. Fire insurance also will be difficult to obtain.

Landscaping

Large tree branches overhanging roof of house or garage can damage roof covering and prevent rainwater from drying under them. Trees or shrubs near foundation can damage wall or cause seepage into foundation. Termites nest in dead trees and shrubs so remove immediately and never burn in fireplace. If termites found outside, have house and garage checked by exterminating company.

Driveway

Concrete driveway: Look for cracks or erosion. If badly deteriorated, needs replacement which can be costly.

Blacktop-covered driveway: Look for cracks. Small cracks can be patched by homeowner. Blacktop should be sealed annually by homeowner. Badly damaged blacktop will need costly repair.

Streetwalk and Walkways

Look for cracks or erosion. See if tree roots have lifted and cracked concrete which is tripping hazard. Repair immediately to prevent lawsuit in case of injury. Size of repairs, or replacement, will determine cost.

Front Entrance Steps

Usually brick, or concrete and brick-constructed. Look for cracks in concrete, and for cracks, spalling, or missing bricks. If badly deteriorated, will be costly to replace. See if sidewalls are out of plumb, also costly to repair. Be sure handrail is anchored securely and see if it is rusted, or paint is peeling. Add handrail for elderly and disabled, if not present.

Central Air Conditioning

Air conditioning unit consists of compressor, condenser coil, and evaporator coil. Freon® used as refrigerant. Refrigerant piping connects to compressor outside of house. Name plate on air conditioning unit gives capacity, power rating, etc.

When inspecting unit, be sure that box with disconnect switch conforms to box stated on name plate on air conditioning unit. It must match specification exactly.

Usually has five- to seven-year warranty. Unit should be covered during winter to increase life expectancy. If inspecting during summer, see how long unit takes to cool house. Should feel cooling effects in about five minutes.

5
Last Bits of Information and Advice

INSECT INFESTATION AND WOOD-DECAYING FUNGUS

Termites

There are two main types of termites, subterranean and non-subterranean termites. Subterranean termites require access to the ground, or to water. Non-subterranean termites live in dry or damp wood and do not need to be in contact with the ground. Subterranean termites are found mostly in the southern half of the United States; however, they are becoming more common in the northern states. Non-subterranean termites are found along the Gulf Coast, especially in Florida, and in states along the southern fringe of the country.

When inspecting for termites, check the area around the foundation walls on the outside and inside (unless the inside wall is covered with paneling or drywall) for evidence of insect infestation. Look for what are called termite tubes (see illustration W). These tubes are dirt tunnels which have been constructed by the termites. These tubes can be seen coming up out of the soil and ascending to the sill plate of the house. Since subterranean termites need moisture, this tube has been constructed by them to make it possible for them to ascend to the sill plate. While you're examining the basement or cellar, check the wood sill plate wher-

ever it is visible. Bring a flashlight for better visibility and a screwdriver to poke the sill plate in order to find any places where it is decayed. Look for piles of sawdust around the sill plate and wood members. Also, look for evidence of treatment in the basement or cellar floor. Treatment is evident in a concrete floor if you see holes in the floor slab that have been refilled. They were refilled after the chemicals were injected into the soil below the slab. This same kind of evidence of treatment is visible in masonry walls and on the exterior concrete around the perimeter of the house.

Ask the owner if the house has been treated for termites and ask to see the termite certificate that was given to the owner after the treatment was completed. Be sure that the guarantee passes on to the new owner and that it covers recurring problems. Examine the condition of the wood joists where they are exposed to be certain that the treatment was effective and that the wood joists are strong. Check for termite infestation even if termite shields have been installed. These shields are not always effective, especially if they have not been installed properly.

If the wood has already been infested by termites, look for tunnels in the wood and specks of earth and excrement on it. Termites may or may not be present in the damaged wood when you view it

- 49 -

since they may have already left it, or they may be dormant in it. Also look for a pile of wings on the window sill which is another indication of termite infestation. Winged termites swarm in the spring and fall and then lose their wings when they nest in the wood. Both tunnels and piles of wings are sure signs that termites have already infested the wood, or are in the process of doing so. In any case, a termite exterminating firm is going to have to be called to eliminate them; then any damage they may have caused will have to be repaired.

While inspecting the outside of the house, make sure that the soil around the house slopes away from it and that the soil is not higher than the exposed section of foundation wall. If the soil is higher, it may be up against the wood siding or the sill plate. This creates an open invitation for termite infestation, so it should be corrected immediately. While you're still outside, also look under the deck, or open porch, for any evidence of termites. If there is a steel cellar door, check the wood framing around it for termite infestation.

If you find termites and the house has not been treated, then it is going to have to be treated by a certified termite exterminating company before you purchase it. A reliable firm should be hired because it is important not to let the vapors from the chemicals into the house since they are very toxic. Vapors from the chemical treatment can get into the house through a variety of ways such as a careless injection of the chemicals into the living areas. These vapors also can come from the air ducts located under the basement floor slab, if the basement floor slab is treated near these air ducts. When the forced-air system is turned on, the vapors are then sent into the living area from the basement. Another way for the vapors to get into the living areas occurs when the exterminating company sprays the soil and/or wood in the crawl space and those vapors then travel up from the crawl space contaminating the living area. To prevent any contamination, these chemicals should never be sprayed indoors. As a matter of fact, some localities have made surface spraying illegal because of the toxic nature of these vapors. Again,

hire a reliable, experienced exterminating company that will handle these chemicals knowledgeably.

In addition to termites, there are two other types of insects which can destroy wood to look for during an inspection, namely powder post beetles and carpenter ants. Look for them in the same places as you did for termites; however, there are different indications of their presence.

Powder Post Beetles

If you see borings in the wood framing members, you are probably looking at powder post beetle infestation. Usually these beetles make many tiny holes in the wood as they leave it. These holes are about the diameter of pencil lead and they give the wood the appearance of destruction as you would see from bird-shot. An exterminating firm will have to be called to eliminate them before you purchase the property.

Carpenter Ants

If you see piles of coarse sawdust outside of the wood framing members while you're inspecting the house, you are looking at infestation caused by carpenter ants. These ants nest in the wood. Generally they can be found in soft wood. Look for carpenter ants in places in the house where there is high humidity, since it is a condition they favor. Again, an exterminating firm is going to have to be hired before you purchase the house.

Wood-Decaying Fungus

Often this type of decay occurs if there is insufficient ventilation in the cellar or basement. It also occurs if the soil is not pitched away from the house properly resulting in poor drainage around the property. This wood decaying fungus also grows on construction lumber that has been buried in the soil under a house, where a house has a roof with an overhang but gutters have not been installed, and in an attic that is not properly ventilated.

The fungi that grow in any of these conditions discolor the wood and, in some cases, even destroy the wood's fiber content. These wood-decaying fungi can soften the wood, make it spongy, cause it to crack, or even to crumble. When viewed, some of these fungi look like mushrooms on the wood.

INSULATION

After you've purchased a house, you may decide that you want to insulate it, or that you want to add to the existing insulation. If you decide to do this, remember that heat not only rises but also moves in a direction from hot to cold. Homeowners mistakenly assume that if they've insulated the attic well, they are automatically saving energy and the rest of the house is fine as is; however, this is not the case. For instance, if there is a basement or cellar below the living area that is unheated, during the wintertime heat is lost from the living area which is heated to the basement or cellar which is not. To prevent this heat loss, put insulation between the floor joists below the living area and be sure that the vapor barrier on the insulation faces up toward the living area. Also, before finishing a basement or cellar with paneling or drywall, insulate the basement or cellar walls to keep heat from being lost through them.

If you buy an old house, remember that most of them do not have insulation in the wall cavities. When you plan to make a major renovation including the removal of plaster from the walls, insulate the wall cavities with roll-type insulation while they are exposed. If the planned renovation is not extensive but you still want to insulate the wall cavities, then have insulation pumped into them through the outside walls. To do this job, a number of holes are made in the outside walls and special equipment is used to pump the insulation into the wall cavities. Afterwards, the holes are sealed completely to prevent water entry and heat loss. If the house is covered with wood siding, pieces of the wood siding are removed, holes are

made at certain distances around the exterior and insulation is pumped into the wall cavities through these holes. The pieces of wood siding that were removed are replaced to prevent water entry into the house and damage to the insulation. If the house is stucco-covered, holes are drilled into the stucco and the insulation is pumped through these holes into the wall cavities. Again, the holes must be sealed completely to prevent water entry and damage to the insulation. Unless you know how to handle the special equipment used to pump insulation into wall cavities, it is best to hire a reliable contractor to do this job for you.

Houses that are balloon-frame constructed (see illustrations O and Q) usually do not have fire-stopping framed into the walls. Newer houses, depending upon the locality and its building code, usually have fire-stopping built into the structure. As a result, it is easier to pump insulation into a balloon-frame constructed house than houses with fire-stopping framed in them. The fire-stopping blocks the flow of insulation into the wall cavities making additional holes necessary to minimize voids of insulation in the wall cavities.

If you see that holes have been made in the house you're inspecting, ask the owner what kind of insulation is used and whether or not it is fire-rated. As noted in the section on the attic in Chapter Three, anywhere from 6″ to 12″ of insulation is adequate, depending upon the height and size of the attic as well as the locality in which the house is situated. One word of caution, though, do not overinsulate your house, or make it too airtight. Airborne gases, pollutants, and irritants associated with everyday living are not able to escape to the outside if the house is too tightly insulated. A house must "breathe" if it is to function properly.

When considering the type of insulation to use in your house, check the fire-resistance of each type as well as the insulation's resistance to vermin. The effect of moisture on the insulation usually dictates where it should be used in the house. All insulation loses its R value to some extent when it becomes wet, but it's especially bad to let fiberglass insulation get even slightly wet. The higher the insulation's R value, the greater resistance it has to heat flow so this factor must be weighed carefully when choosing an insulation. Review the manufacturers' specifications to compare all of this information and for their recommendations on how and where it should be used. The decision of what insulation to use is going to be based on where you want to put it in your house. For example, if your house has a damp basement, or a wet crawl space, then before insulation is pumped into the walls, you must first resolve this problem of dampness. Also, it's helpful to get recommendations from an insulation contractor, if you hire one to handle this job for you.

ASBESTOS

In many older houses, the insulation found around the boiler, the steam pipe, and the flue pipe that goes to the chimney may be hazardous. Depending upon its age, the insulation may be made with asbestos, a known carcinogen. The asbestos is going to have to be encapsulated or removed, depending upon its condition, by a certified asbestos removal company. This is absolutely not a job for the homeowner to undertake.

Asbestos was used extensively in many building products until the 1970s. Houses were constructed with asbestos shingles on the outside and asbestos floor and ceiling tiles on the inside. Asbestos was even in many of the patching compounds used to repair cracks in walls and ceilings.

When inspecting the inside of the house, look for old ceiling tiles or vinyl floor tiles since these products may contain asbestos, although not all older tiles do. If you are planning a major renovation in a room with any of these old products, have a sample of these products tested for asbestos before you proceed with the renovation. If the test proves positive, then you should hire a certified asbestos removal company to remove these materials before any part of the renovation is started.

As noted earlier in this chapter, if you find that the wall cavities in a house are filled with insulation, then you should ask the owner what material is used as insulation, or have the insulation tested, if the owner doesn't know. If it is found to be asbestos, or a formaldehyde product, these are known carcinogens and you should be aware of their danger.

FIREPLACES AND CHIMNEYS

If the house you're inspecting is more than 100 years old and it has a working fireplace, look up the chimney flue with a flashlight to see if the chimney is lined. Also look to see if a great deal of creosote has built up on the chimney walls. In many older houses, chimneys are not lined because liners usually were not required when the houses were built. Due to the age of the chimney and its frequent use over the years, the chimney probably will need to have a liner installed, and the brickwork may have to be rehabilitated. Deteriorated brickwork is a potential fire hazard, so a fireplace professional is going to have to be hired to do this work correctly in order to make the fireplace and chimney safe for use. Even if the brickwork is sound, the chimney will need to be cleaned if any creosote has built up in it because creosote buildup is a potential fire hazard, too.

While inspecting the flue in the fireplace, check the damper to make sure it opens and closes properly. You are going to want it to close tightly during the winter months to keep cold air out of the house when the fireplace is not in use. If you can get onto the roof during the inspection, check the construction of the chimneys used for the heating system and for the fireplaces. If the chimneys are lined, usually you can see them because the liners extend past the masonry section of the chimneys.

Whether the masonry chimney is being used for the central heating system or for the fireplaces, you should examine the chimney to make sure that it is clear of all products of combustion as well as creosote. If there is a cleanout door at the bottom of the chimney, look to see if the chimney is clean.

While you're on the roof, check the integrity of the masonry above the roof line. Be sure that the chimney is plumb, that it is not tilting, and that it is not falling apart. If the masonry is deteriorating, or if the chimney is out of plumb, it is going to have to be repaired and this can be a very costly project. You also can anticipate a costly project if the chimney has to be lined, or even if the existing liner has to be repaired. This work should only be done by a professional and this professional's fee will not be cheap; however, this is not work for the do-it-yourselfer.

If the chimney you're inspecting is at the side of the house, check the joint that is formed between the chimney and the house wall. Look for any indications that the chimney is pulling away from the wall. Look to see if the distance between the joint formed by the house and the chimney increases as the chimney ascends to the roof line. If it does, it may indicate that the chimney's footing is failing. If the chimney you're inspecting is free-standing, look to see that it is plumb and check the brickwork to be sure that it is not cracked or deteriorated (see illustration X).

It's also important to check the condition of the mortar in the chimney. If it is crumbling or wet, there may be leaks from water entry, or sections of the mortar may be missing entirely. This condition is a potential fire hazard because sparks could escape from the chimney, go into the wood framing, and ignite a fire. This condition should be repaired immediately.

If the fireplaces in the house you've purchased have been sealed for many years but you now want to use them, you will first have to hire a fireplace professional to inspect their condition inside and out. The fireplace and chimney may be so old and neglected that they will have to be rebuilt entirely before they can be used. This is going to be a costly rehabilitation project, but it is absolutely necessary for the safe and proper use of the fireplace. Remember that even if the fireplace has a liner and even if it has been used recently, you should call a

fireplace professional to inspect it completely and to clean it thoroughly before you use it.

FIRE ESCAPES

If fire escapes are attached to the building you're inspecting, examine the condition of the iron work. Look for rust, which means that the fire escapes will need to be painted. If you see extensive rust and corrosion, examine the location where the structural members of the fire escape's baskets are anchored into the wall of the building to be sure that they are anchored securely. Check the condition of the platform steel of the baskets. If there is a ladder that ascends to the roof, check its structural integrity and make sure it is anchored securely into the roof. Remember that in order to keep fire escapes in good condition, they are going to have to be scraped and painted on a regular basis. Fire escapes should never be neglected, or allowed to become structurally unsafe, because they are in place to save lives. As a matter of fact, in some localities, fire escapes that have been left unpainted and rusted are considered to be violations of the building code.

SMOKE DETECTORS

An inexpensive and simple thing that you can do to keep your family safe from fires is to install smoke detectors in your home. Either install battery-operated smoke detectors yourself, or have them connected to your electrical system by a licensed electrician. You should install a smoke detector on the ceilings in each level of your home, specifically near sleeping areas, outside the kitchen, on the center of the hallway ceiling, and on the ceiling of a basement or cellar stairway. Since basements or cellars usually house the furnace, the hot water tank, and often the washer/dryer, it's particularly important to install a smoke detector at the stairway in case any of these systems malfunction and cause a fire.

The kitchen is not a good location for a smoke detector because the heat and smoke given off from cooking will set it off frequently. Keep smoke detectors out of bathrooms too because the heat and steam in these rooms can trigger many false alarms.

Remember to change the batteries in the smoke detector every couple of months to be sure that it will always be able to function in case of a fire. It's also a good idea to be sure to test your smoke detectors, according to the manufacturer's instructions, so that you know it will work in case of a fire.

WATER SOFTENERS

Water softeners are used to treat mineral deposits found in hard water. Depending upon your locality, the water may contain rust and/or a variety of minerals such as calcium, magnesium, and iron. Hard water can be detected when you see a rust-colored ring around the bathtub. Water softeners treat the hard water by substituting salt for mineral deposits.

Some water softening units are connected to the hot water plumbing so that only the water being used for bathing and washing is treated. In this way, the added salt is kept out of the drinking water so that individuals who need to limit their intake of sodium are not affected.

SEPTIC TANKS

In houses that are not served by a city sewer or town sewer system, a septic tank is used to collect sewage and dispose of it. The solid waste is collected in these tanks and disintegrated by bacteria. It is important not to send chemicals, oils, grease, fats, or thick paper through this kind of system. The septic tank system is composed of a tank, pipes, manholes, and a drainage field. If thick paper is sent into this system, it clogs the pipes. If chemicals, oils, fats, or grease are flushed into the system, they destroy the bacteria that disintegrates the solid wastes. Once the bacteria are destroyed, the solid wastes can no longer be disintegrated. The inlet and outlet pipes will become clogged, and odors and gases will build up in the house and

eventually in the neighborhood. If the system is not repaired or replaced, sewage will back up into the house over an extended period of time.

If the property you're inspecting has a septic tank system installed, hire a professional to make sure that it is functioning properly. Remember that the tank should be checked and cleaned at least once a year, or according to the manufacturer's instructions.

TESTING THE EFFICIENCY OF THE FURNACE/BOILER

If your home, or the one you're inspecting, has an oil-fired heating system in operation, or even an old one that was converted from coal to oil, you may want to learn the efficiency of the furnace/boiler. The oil service company that has been supplying fuel can conduct a series of tests to determine its efficiency at the time of combustion.

Since a proper draft is a basic requirement for efficient combustion, the oil service company will start by checking the draft. The draft determines how much air is being supplied for combustion and how fast the combustion gases are flowing through the furnace/boiler. If the draft is too high, the stack temperature will increase. To conduct all of the tests, the oil service company will first make a $\frac{1}{4}''$ hole in the flue pipe. A draft gauge is inserted through this hole for the draft test. Since the amount of carbon dioxide is reduced by the amount of draft in the flue pipe, a sample of flue gas also is taken to see how much carbon dioxide is present.

A stack thermometer is inserted into the flue pipe to determine the stack temperature. A high stack temperature may indicate that the draft is too high, the furnace/boiler is over-firing, a great deal of soot has collected in the furnace/boiler, or even that the furnace/boiler is undersized. If the furnace/boiler is very old, it may be difficult to determine the proper stack temperature, so you will have to rely on the oil service company's recommendation.

There are two more tests to be done at this time. First the oil pressure is checked with a pressure gauge to see if the oil pump is operating properly. Also a smoke test is conducted to measure and analyze the smoke content in the flue pipe. Poor results of the smoke test may indicate that there is a poor draft, that the fuel–air mixture is not in proper proportion, or that the combustion chamber is defective. There can even be more serious problems present which the oil service company will explain to you. If the furnace/boiler is found to be very inefficient, you may have to install a brand new heating system which will cut your fuel cost and improve heating throughout your home.

RADON

Radon is an odorless, invisible, radioactive gas which is produced by the breakdown of uranium. High concentrations of radon can be found in soil and rock containing uranium, shale, phosphate, or granite. If you are inspecting a house that is built on a landfill, especially one used as a dumping site for industrial wastes which may have contained elements from uranium or phosphate mixing, you may be looking at a house with a radon problem, or one with at least a potential radon problem.

As radon gas accumulates, it seeps into the house through a variety of possible entry paths. The amount of radon in a house depends upon the type of construction utilized to build the house as well as the amount of radon in the soil below it. Exposure to radon can cause an increased risk of developing lung cancer, so it is a serious concern. A detailed study of the effects of radon can be obtained from your local or state environmental agency.

Radon can enter the house through dirt floors in the cellar, cracks in the concrete floor slab, or cracks in the foundation walls. If the house has a pit which is being used to house a sump pump, and if there are area floor drains in the basement, radon can enter through small cracks in the pit or in the floor drains. If the house is built on a block-constructed foundation and there are cracks in it, radon can enter into the house through these cracks.

Remember that not all houses have radon in them. As a matter of fact, the greater majority of houses built in the United States do not appear to have a problem with radon gas. If you want to be sure that the house you are purchasing, or for that matter have already purchased, is radon free, there are two ways to test for the presence of this gas. If you want to do it yourself, you can buy a radon testing kit from a local hardware store. Follow directions on the kit to expose it to the air in your house for the period of time specified and than send it to the laboratory for analysis. If you don't want to do the test yourself, you can hire a private testing company to do it for you.

There also are ways to prevent radon gas from seeping into your home. Seal any cracks that you find in the foundation floor slab, in the foundation walls, in the pit and in the area drains. Add ventilation in your basement or cellar to increase air flow and to disperse gases collecting there and, if you have a crawl space, keep it well ventilated at all times. If you hire a private testing company, discuss ways to eliminate radon seepage into your home with the company while the test is being performed.

ALUMINUM WIRING

As stated in Chapter One on electrical service, aluminum wiring is a potential fire hazard and its use is prohibited in some local and state electrical codes. There are many different properties inherent in aluminum wiring that make it inferior to copper wiring. For instance, aluminum wire's conductivity is not as great as copper wire's for the same given size. In other words, #8 copper wire can be used for 40-ampere service, but #8 aluminum wire can only carry 30-ampere service. Aluminum wire also has a lower overcurrent protection. For example, the overcurrent protection for a #12 A.W.G. copper wire is 20-amperes while the #12 A.W.G. aluminum wire, or copper-clad aluminum wire, is only 15-amperes.

Aluminum wire also has other characteristics that make it a poor substitute for copper wire. Aluminum conductors have a greater resistance than copper conductors in the same given size and this causes voltage to drop sharply. Also aluminum wire contracts and expands to a greater degree than copper. This expansion and contraction results in poor connections on aluminum wire. As soon as aluminum wire is exposed to air, it oxidizes and this oxidized surface also results in a poor connection.

Usually switches and receptacle connectors are marked to indicate what wire should be used with each of them. If a 15- or 20-ampere device has no markings, use only copper. If it is marked with "CU-AL," use only copper wire. If it is marked "CO-ALR," the National Electrical Code says that the conductor permitted can be aluminum, copper, or copper-clad aluminum for 15- or 20-ampere receptacles and switches; however, if you encounter aluminum wire, I recommend that you have a licensed electrician change it to copper. Whether the wire is copper, aluminum, or copper-clad aluminum, it cannot be used in a combination of materials in the same connector. In other words, only one material should be run to it.

SOME TIPS FOR THE HOME BUYER

1. If you see burned-out fuses near the fuse box, usually this indicates that the electrical system is being overloaded frequently and that the electrical service for this house is inadequate.

2. Examine the area around the burner in the furnace to see if it is clean and if the flame is blue. If not, the boiler has to be cleaned and adjusted by the plumber or the utility company. Make a visual inspection only, don't touch anything.

3. Depending upon the local code in your area, three-family and larger buildings usually must have the boiler housed in a fire-rated structure.

4. If the house you're about to purchase was left empty before it was sold and you're buying it during the cold winter months, check the plumbing carefully in case there was a freeze-out in the house. Look for leaks and water stains to indicate where the plumbing was damaged during the freeze-out.

5. Always take note of the slope of the grade around the property. The soil should slope away from the house for proper drainage (see illustration R). This helps to prevent water entry through the foundation and into the cellar or basement.

6. When inspecting a bathroom, look to see if any grout is missing around the tiles and at the base of the tub. Remember to regrout these areas after you've purchased the property to prevent water entry and the damage it can cause to the structure below.

7. If your garage door operates with an electrically operated opener, make sure that the door stops automatically when it encounters an obstacle such as a pet, toy, or child.

8. If the washing machine installed in the basement is not vented, it is a violation of the building code. In some localities back-flow valves also are required on the water lines to prevent water from backing up into the drinking water system.

9. Some local codes require that any beams or joists which have been damaged by fire must be replaced, even if there is only ⅛″ of char on them. You'll have to find out what code applies in your area, if you encounter this condition.

10. If the house you're inspecting has suspended ceiling tiles installed, lift up a few of the tiles to check the condition of the original ceilings that these tiles are covering. Sometimes these tiles are hiding badly damaged plaster or drywall ceilings which are going to have to be repaired.

11. During the inspection, turn on everything you can including the heating system and air conditioning in the summertime. You don't want to find out that something doesn't work after you've purchased the house. However, don't try the air conditioning during the winter because you could damage the unit.

12. While you're inspecting the interior of the house, look at the skylights for any water stains which may indicate water entry. Also, while on the roof, make sure the skylights are sealed properly to prevent water entry.

13. If there is a very high set of masonry steps at the front of the house, look underneath it for any evidence of seepage of rainwater coming in through the steps.

14. If a dryer has been installed in the basement, make sure it is vented to the outside to prevent lint buildup in the basement. Remember that lint is very flammable.

15. If an addition has been built onto the house you're inspecting, ask the owner if it was done legally, that is, if appropriate building permits were secured. If not, the bank may not want to approve your mortgage application because the addition would be an illegal one and a violation of the building code.

16. If you see that a flexible gas connector has been connected to the hot water heater, be sure that it is changed to pipe that is suitable for gas service before you purchase the house. In many localities, this flexible gas connector, which is used for appliances, is a violation of the building code when used in this application.

17. Bathrooms and toilet facilities that do not have windows installed will need to have mechanical ventilating systems put in place for proper ventilation.

18. The use of extension cords in a house usually means that there are not enough outlets in the house. In many areas, the use of extension cords is a violation of the electrical code.

19. The soil in some areas may have a high clay deposit. In areas with a high clay deposit, the water drains poorly away from the house's foundation and its footings. As a result, a seepage problem could develop and the foundation and footings could even be weakened.

20. The solder that joins the copper tubing used for drinking water may contain lead. To find out if this condition exists in the house you're inspecting, you will have to have the drinking water tested for the presence of lead. If it tests positive, then the copper tubing will have to be replaced, presuming, of course, that you know the water main is not lead.

21. If dissimilar materials are joined together in a plumbing system (galvanized, copper), the contact of these dissimilar materials causes corrosion of the plumbing at the point of contact. Look for corrosion on the surface of the plumbing for evidence of this condition.

22. Some newer homes have a grounding electrode system instead of a ground run to the water main. If you're looking at a newer house, ask the owner if it has this system.

SOME TIPS FOR THE HOMEOWNER

1. Always use good grades of caulk for all of your caulking needs. They last longer and do a better job of preventing leaks.

2. Make sure that areaways around basement windows are kept clean to prevent fires from starting in the debris, and to prevent flooding and insect and rodent infestation.

3. If your house is heated with a steam system, change the air valves at the radiators and at the steam header. New valves will make the system work more efficiently.

4. If you decide to add a deck to your house, do not attach it to the house where water entry

can become a problem. Make it self-standing unless it is a high deck that needs to be braced.

5. When finishing a basement, add insulation to the foundation walls to keep the basement warmer in the winter and cooler in the summer than it would be without insulation.

6. Paint metal railings and fences often to prevent rust as well as needless repair and replacement.

7. If the roots from the tree in front of your house grow into your main sewer line, purchase a root killer from a plumbing supply store and use it as frequently as directed. These crystals will kill the roots in the sewer line that can cause a blockage after several months of growth.

8. If you have a manually operated, roll-up type garage door, grease the rollers every year to make lifting it a lot easier for you and your family.

9. If there is an area drain outside of your home, usually it would be in the back, flush it with water two or three times a year to clear it of any leaves or soil. This debris can cause a blockage, and during a heavy rainstorm water will back up into basement windows that are low to the ground.

10. Check every radiator in the house regularly for leaking valves. Sometimes a new valve will be needed, or the old one will need new packing.

11. It's a good idea to change all outlets to the ground-fault interrupter type, but definitely change those in the bathrooms and kitchen and outside such as near the pool, in the garage, etc.

12. If the electrical panel box is enclosed in a wood cabinet, or is hidden behind paneling, remove the cabinet or paneling so that you have easy access to the panel box at all times.

13. Insulate any part of the piping on the cold water line that you see "sweating."

14. Cut away any tree branches that hang onto your roof since they can damage the roof covering. Also remove all dead trees and shrubs to prevent insect infestation in them and, eventually, into your home.

15. Don't discard any sand, cement, latex paint, etc., down the drains because they can accumulate and eventually cause a blockage.

16. Keep exterior fences around your property freshly painted and replace them as needed. If you live on a hill and there is a brick retaining wall around the lower section of your property, make sure you keep it structurally intact. Replacement would be costly but necessary to prevent soil erosion, or water damage to anything below the retaining wall.

17. Always caulk any cracks as they occur in your concrete steps and repoint loose bricks where mortar has fallen out from between them. This kind of regular maintenance could save you costly replacement of your concrete steps and brickwork.

18. Clean your kitchen trap regularly to prevent a blockage from grease and food scraps. Use paper towels to clean oils and food scraps from your dishes instead of letting them go down the drain.

19. As part of regular maintenance for your forced-air heating system, install a new air filter annually.

20. If you use your gas barbecue often, clean any grease that collects in the bottom below the charcoal on a monthly basis. This grease can ignite a flash fire if the gas leaks, or if there is a similar malfunction of the barbecue.

21. For safety's sake it's a good idea to install a smoke detector in the living area near the interior garage's fire-rated door. If the car happens to catch on fire, a smoke detector will warn you immediately.

22. To reduce your air conditioning bills, install an attic fan to vent hot air out of the attic and to assist in cooling the house.

23. Have screens installed on your gutters to cut down on the amount of leaves and other debris that collects in them. This debris could eventually cause damage to the leaders, and even to the house, because of blockages it can create.

24. If your heating system suddenly comes on during the summer, it could mean that the thermostat for the heating system is malfunctioning and that a new one is going to have to be installed.

25. If you have a house with old hardwood floors that were face-nailed when they were installed, be careful if you decide to sand these floors. The nail heads may be loose or could become loose during the sanding and they will need to be renailed.

26. Call your plumber or utility company every year to clean your boiler and to make sure that the chimney is clean.

27. A homeowner needs a few basic tools, even if he or she is not a full-fledged do-it-yourselfer. Hammers, screwdrivers, a saw, a drill, and wrenches can come in handy for everyday repairs, or at least to keep things together until the repairman comes.

28. If you decide to remove your oil-fired heating system after you've purchased the house, the fuel storage tank also will have to be removed. Once this has been done, make sure that the inlet pipe on the outside of your house is sealed completely. This will prevent the oil service company from mistakenly pumping oil into your basement. Don't laugh, I know of several instances where this has occurred.

SUMMARY

Termites

Types: Subterranean: Require access to ground or water, found mostly in southern U.S., becoming more common in northern states. Non-subterranean: Live in dry or damp wood, found along Gulf Coast and southern fringe of United States.

Look for termite tubes on foundation walls coming up out of the soil and ascending up to the sill plate. Check the sill plate wherever possible in basement by poking it with screwdriver to find decay. Look for piles of sawdust around sill plate and wood members. Look for holes that have been refilled inside and outside which are evidence of treatment.

If treated, ask owner to see certificate to determine guarantee. See that treatment was effective by checking exposed wood joists. Look for termites even if termite shields have been installed; sometimes installation is poorly done.

Termites may or may not be present at time of inspection. Look for pile of wings on window sills. If you find tunnels or wings, call exterminating company to treat. All damaged wood must be repaired.

Be sure soil outside is not higher than foundation wall, up against wood siding or sill plate. This is open invitation for termites. Look under deck and open porch for termites, also around wood frame on steel cellar door.

If house needs treatment, get reliable firm that will keep toxic vapors out of house. Chemicals should not be sprayed indoors. In some localities, surface spraying is illegal.

Powder Post Beetles

Look for many tiny holes in wood, diameter of pencil lead. Wood has appearance of destruction from bird-shot. Call exterminating company if holes are found. Look in same places as for termites.

Carpenter Ants

Look for piles of coarse sawdust outside of the wood framing members. Ants like to nest in soft wood and in places with high humidity. Call exterminating company, if found.

Wood-Decaying Fungus

Caused by insufficient ventilation in cellar, or poor drainage around property. Fungus also grows on construction lumber buried in soil, in house without gutters and with roof that has overhang, or in poorly ventilated attic. Wood discolored and fiber content destroyed. Wood may be soft, spongy, cracked, or crumbled. Some fungi look like mushrooms.

Insulation

Heat not only rises, but also moves in directions from hot to cold, so insulate unheated basements as well as attic. Insulate walls before finishing them and between floor joists below living area.

Most old houses don't have insulation in wall cavities. During major renovation, use roll-type insulation when wall cavities exposed. If not renovating, have insulation pumped into wall cavities through holes in outside walls. If covered with wood siding, first remove pieces, make holes, then pump insulation into wall cavities. Replace pieces of wood siding. If house stucco-covered, holes made in stucco, then sealed after insulation pumped in. Best to hire reliable contractor to do job.

Easier to pump insulation into balloon-frame construction house than in house with fire-stopping built into wall cavities. Additional holes will be needed to minimize voids in insulation.

If insulation pumped into house, ask owner type of insulation used and if it is fire-rated. Do not overinsulate house and trap airborne gases, pollutants, and irritants in it. House must "breathe."

Check fire-resistance of insulation and effect of moisture on it when choosing type to use. Insulation's R value lost to some degree by moisture, worse with fiberglass insulation. Use insulation with high R value and good vermin-resistance. Review manufacturers' specifications and contractor's recommendations to pick type.

Asbestos

In many older homes, insulation around boiler, steam pipe, and flue may be asbestos, which is carcinogen. Certified asbestos removal company must encapsulate or remove it, not homeowner.

Asbestos used extensively before 1970s for asbestos shingles, ceiling tiles, and floor tiles. Also in patching compounds used to repair cracks in walls and ceilings.

Inside house, look for old ceiling tiles or vinyl floor tiles, but not all contain asbestos. Before major renovation, have samples tested. If asbestos present, hire certified asbestos removal company before any part of renovation started.

If insulation in wall cavities, ask owner what material was used, or if not known, have sample tested. Asbestos, or a formaldehyde product, is a known carcinogen.

Fireplaces and Chimneys

If house is more than 100 years old with working fireplace, see if chimney is lined and if creosote has built up in it. Liners were not required when older houses were built. Have liner installed and brickwork rehabilitated before using. Deteriorated brickwork and creosote are potential fire hazards and must be taken care of before fireplace used.

Make sure damper in flue opens and closes properly. It must close tightly in winter to keep cold out when not in use. When on roof, look for chimney liner to extend past masonry section of chimney.

Whether chimney is used for central heating or fireplaces, be sure it is clear of all products of combustion. Look into cleanout door at bottom of chimney to see it is cleaned. While on roof, check integrity of chimney to see it is cleaned. While on roof, check integrity of masonry, be sure chimney not tilted or falling apart. Will be costly repair if masonry deteriorated, chimney out of plumb, or liner needs repair or replacement. Professional must do repair, not homeowner.

Chimney at side of house, check joint formed between chimney and house wall for separation. Footing for chimney failing if space increases as chimney ascends to roof. Chimney free-standing, be sure is plumb, not cracked or deteriorated.

Be sure mortar in chimney is not wet, crumbling, or missing entirely. Potential fire hazard and must be repaired immediately.

Before using fireplaces that have been sealed for many years, hire fireplace professional to restore as needed. Total rehabilitation will be costly. Even if chimney is lined and recently used, have professional clean and check before using.

Fire Escapes

Look for rust which means needs to be painted. If badly rusted and corroded, be sure structural members of baskets anchored securely into walls. Check ladder's integrity and make sure anchored securely. Paint regularly or may be a violation of building code.

Smoke Detectors

Install battery-operated smoke detectors, or have licensed electrician connect them to electrical system. Put on ceilings in each level of house, near sleeping areas, outside kitchen, near basement stairway, and on center of hallway ceiling. Do not install in kitchens or bathrooms. Change batteries every two months and test according to manufacturer's instructions.

Water Softeners

Used to treat mineral deposits in hard water. Minerals present if rust-colored ring seen around tub. Substitutes salt for minerals in water used for bathing or washing. Salt kept out of drinking water for those who must limit sodium in diets.

Septic Tanks

Used to collect and dispose of sewage in houses not served by city or town sewer system. Solid waste disintegrated by bacteria. Keep chemicals, oils, grease, fats, and thick paper out of system. Paper clogs pipes, and chemicals, etc., destroy bacteria, which could cause odors, gases, sewage to back up in house. Before buying house, have professional check to be sure functions properly. Tank must be checked and cleaned according to manufacturer's instructions.

Testing and Efficiency of the Furnace/Boiler

House with oil-fired heating system, or one converted from coal to oil, have oil service company conduct tests to determine efficiency. Tests done for draft, presence of carbon dioxide, stack temperature, oil pressure, and smoke. If not efficient, need new heating system installed to cut fuel costs and improve heating in house.

Radon

Odorless, invisible, radioactive gas produced by breakdown of uranium in soil and rock, which is under house built on landfill, especially one used as dumping site for industrial wastes.

Amount of radon in house depends upon type of construction and how much is in soil below it. High risk of developing lung cancer from radon exposure. Get details from local environmental agencies.

Radon enters house through cracks in floor slab, foundation walls, pit, or floor drains.

Most houses in United States don't have radon problem. To be sure, get do-it-yourself testing kit from hardware store, or call private testing company.

To prevent radon from seeping into house, seal all cracks and add ventilation to basement and crawl space. Discuss other ways with private testing company, if hired.

Aluminum Wiring

Inferior to copper wiring for many reasons. Use prohibited by some local and state electrical codes.

Aluminum wire of same size carries lower amperage, also has greater resistance which reduces voltage. Aluminum makes poor connections due to greater expansion and oxidation as soon as exposed to air.

Switches and receptacle connectors marked to indicate what type of wire to use. If no markings, use only copper conductors. Never use combination of materials.

Appendix

HOW TO USE THE HOME INSPECTION CHECKLIST

First take a little time to familiarize yourself with the content and style of the checklist. Review it before you go to inspect a house so that it's fresh in your mind. Use a separate checklist for each of the houses you inspect; you can make as many copies as you need. After you've completed all of the inspections, compare the checklists page by page, looking for the house with the fewest major problems and with a moderate amount of minor work. Then fill in the comparison checklist on page 85. If you've indicated that there's a major problem in a house you'd still like to purchase, have an expert in that particular field review the problem for you. You want the professional to tell you what work is involved and how much it will cost to resolve the problem to your satisfaction. If there are lots of minor problems, get estimates of the costs, then decide if you can afford to have the work done for you, or if you can do the work yourself.

Remember there is no set formula for picking the house you're going to buy; however, it is essential that you understand what work, if any, is involved and how much that work will cost. You also should know if all or part of the work can wait until you have the money and/or time to handle it, or if you

should find another house with fewer anticipated costs. Get as much advice as you can from professionals, friends, relatives, your lawyer, anyone you know who has already dealt with this kind of decision. Take your time to make the decision. Keep looking if you don't feel secure with what you're being advised to do, or even if you're just not sure the house is right for you. Good luck and happy house hunting.

HOW TO USE THE COMPARISON CHECKLIST

After you've inspected all of the houses you're interested in purchasing and you've reviewed the checklists, you may find it helpful to reduce that number to three houses and then to make a general comparison of them. Just mark the box for House #1, House #2, or House #3 where it is most appropriate regarding the statement listed. When you're done, the house with the most marks is the one you will want to consider most seriously. Take note of any boxes that you didn't mark and decide how to resolve that problem. You may need advice from your attorney or from a specific professional in order to decide what to do. If you can resolve any and all of the problems to your satisfaction, you may just have decided on the house you want to buy.

HOME INSPECTION CHECKLIST

Address _____ Age _____

Date _____ Most Recent Rainfall _____

EXTERIOR

Front	OK	OK w/ Minor Work	Major Problems
Brick bulging, spalling, cracking			
Mortar loose, needs repointing			
Lintel needs repair			
Brick sandblasted			
Stucco bulging, cracking			
Stucco needs repainting			
Caulking needed			
Aluminum siding dented, damaged			
Finish wearing off siding			
Aluminum siding loose, not level, missing			
Vinyl siding dented, damaged			
Vinyl siding loose, not level, missing			
Wood siding rotted, damaged, termites			
Wood siding loose, not level, missing			
Wood siding needs refinishing			
Asphalt shingles worn, broken, missing			
Asphalt shingles loose, need replacement			
Asbestos shingles broken, loose, missing			
Asbestos shingles need replacement			
Redwood/cedar not level, loose, damaged			
Cedar siding needs to be refinished			
Holes made in exterior wall for insulation			

REMARKS

Left Side	OK	OK w/ Minor Work	Major Problems
Brick bulging, spalling, cracking			
Mortar loose, needs repointing			
Lintel needs repair			
Brick sandblasted			
Stucco bulging, cracking			
Stucco needs repainting			
Caulking needed			
Aluminum siding dented, damaged			
Finish wearing off siding			
Aluminum siding loose, not level, missing			
Vinyl siding dented, damaged			
Vinyl siding loose, not level, missing			
Wood siding rotted, damaged, termites			
Wood siding loose, not level, missing			
Wood siding needs refinishing			
Asphalt shingles worn, broken, missing			
Asphalt shingles loose, need replacement			
Asbestos shingles broken, loose, missing			
Asbestos shingles need replacement			
Redwood/cedar not level, loose, damaged			
Cedar siding needs to be refinished			
Holes made in exterior wall for insulation			
REMARKS			
Right Side			
Brick bulging, spalling, cracking			
Mortar loose, needs repointing			
Lintel needs repair			
Brick sandblasted			
Stucco bulging, cracking			
Stucco needs repainting			

Right Side, continued	OK	OK w/ Minor Work	Major Problems
Caulking needed			
Aluminum siding dented, damaged			
Finish wearing off siding			
Aluminum siding loose, not level, missing			
Vinyl siding dented, damaged			
Vinyl siding loose, not level, missing			
Wood siding rotted, damaged, termites			
Wood siding loose, not level, missing			
Wood siding needs refinishing			
Asphalt shingles worn, broken, missing			
Asphalt shingles loose, need replacement			
Asbestos shingles broken, loose, missing			
Asbestos shingles need replacement			
Redwood/cedar not level, loose, damaged			
Cedar siding needs refinishing			
Holes made in exterior wall for insulation			
REMARKS			
Rear			
Brick bulging, spalling, cracking			
Mortar loose, needs repointing			
Lintel needs repair			
Brick sandblasted			
Stucco bulging, cracking			
Stucco needs repainting			
Caulking needed			
Aluminum siding dented, damaged			
Finish wearing off siding			
Aluminum siding loose, not level, missing			
Vinyl siding dented, damaged			
Vinyl siding loose, not level, missing			

Rear, continued	OK	OK w/ Minor Work	Major Problems
Wood siding rotted, damaged, termites			
Wood siding loose, not level, missing			
Asphalt shingles worn, broken, missing			
Asphalt shingles loose, need replacement			
Asbestos shingles broken, loose, missing			
Asbestos shingles need replacement			
Redwood/cedar not level, loose, damaged			
Cedar siding needs refinishing			
Holes made in exterior wall for insulation			
REMARKS			
Roofing (House)			
Age of covering			
Asphalt shingles worn, damaged, patched			
Asphalt shingles have more than two layers			
Slate worn, damaged, white stains			
Slate patched, loose			
Terra cotta tile worn, damaged			
Terra cotta tile patched, loose			
Wood shingles worn, damaged			
Wood shingles patched, loose			
Wood shingles not fire-rated			
Roll roofing paper blistered, seams exposed			
Water puddling on flat roof, poor pitch			
Brick chimney broken, leaning			
Joint open between chimney & exterior wall			
Need flashing at chimney, vents, walls			
Roof needs to be recovered			
Parapet wall leaning			
Papapet wall damaged, loose masonry			
Tile coping loose, damaged			

Roofing (House), continued	OK	OK w/ Minor Work	Major Problems
Metal flashing damaged, missing			
REMARKS			
Roofing (Garage)			
Age of covering			
Asphalt shingles worn, damaged, patched			
Asphalt shingles have more than two layers			
Slate worn, damaged, white stains			
Slate patched, loose			
Terra cotta tile worn, damaged			
Terra cotta tile patched, loose			
Wood shingles worn, damaged			
Wood shingles patched, loose			
Wood shingles not fire-rated			
Roll roofing paper blistered, seams exposed			
Water puddling on flat roof, poor pitch			
Roof needs to be recovered			
Need flashing at walls			
Parapet wall leaning			
Parapet wall damaged, loose masonry			
Tile coping loose, damaged			
Metal flashing damaged, missing			
REMARKS			
Gutters and Leaders			
Age of gutters/leaders			
Copper discolored, greenish, damaged			
Galvanized rusted, patched			
Fascia board rotted, damaged, patched			
Need to be cleaned, nailed			
Need to be replaced			

Gutters and Leaders, continued	OK	OK w/ Minor Work	Major Problems
Drain onto foundation wall			
Need to divert water from wall			
Soffits need venting			
Soffits need painting			
Concrete slab cracked, deteriorated			
Concrete slab/splash block needed			
REMARKS			
Front Exterior Door			
Damaged, needs refinishing			
Needs replacement			
Needs weatherstripping			
Trim rotted, missing			
Threshold rotted, missing			
Add locks			
Add storm door			
Jambs rotted, damaged			
Jambs need repainting			
Jambs need replacement			
REMARKS			
Side or Back Exterior Door			
Damaged, needs refinishing			
Needs replacement			
Needs weatherstripping			
Trim rotted, missing			
Threshold rotted, missing			
Add locks			
Add storm door			
Jambs rotted, damaged			
Jambs need repainting			

Side or Back Exterior Door, continued	OK	OK w/ Minor Work	Major Problems
Jambs need replacement			
REMARKS			
Cellar Door			
Damaged, needs refinishing			
Needs replacement			
Add locks			
Jambs rotted, damaged			
Jambs need repainting			
Jambs need replacement			
REMARKS			
Front Windows			
Wood needs repainting			
Sash rotted			
Trim rotted			
Replace broken glass			
Won't open, close easily			
Sash cord/chains broken			
Sills decayed, need replacement			
Insulated glass seal failed			
Need storm windows			
Need energy-efficient windows			
REMARKS			
Left Side Windows			
Wood needs repainting			
Sash rotted			
Trim rotted			
Replace broken glass			

Left Side Windows, continued	OK	OK w/ Minor Work	Major Problems
Won't open, close easily			
Sash cord/chains broken			
Sills decayed, need replacement			
Insulated glass seal failed			
Need storm windows			
Need energy-efficient windows			
REMARKS			
Right Side Windows			
Wood needs repainting			
Sash rotted			
Trim rotted			
Replace broken glass			
Won't open, close easily			
Sash cord/chains broken			
Sills decayed, need replacement			
Insulated glass seal failed			
Need storm windows			
Need energy-efficient windows			
REMARKS			
Rear Windows			
Wood needs repainting			
Sash rotted			
Trim rotted			
Replace broken glass			
Won't open, close easily			
Sash cord/chains broken			
Sills decayed, need replacement			
Insulated glass seal failed			
Need storm windows			

Rear Windows, continued	OK	OK w/ Minor Work	Major Problems
Need energy-efficient windows			
REMARKS			

Front Entrance Steps			
Concrete cracked			
Brick cracked, mortar loose			
Brick or stone needs repointing			
Sidewalls need reconstruction			
Handrail needs painting			
Reanchor handrail			
Replace handrail			
Replace steps			
Repaint wood steps			
Replace wood steps			
REMARKS			

Side or Back Entrance Steps			
Concrete cracked			
Brick cracked, mortar loose			
Brick or stone needs repointing			
Sidewalls need reconstruction			
Handrail needs painting			
Reanchor handrail			
Replace handrail			
Replace steps			
Repaint wood steps			
Replace wood steps			
REMARKS			

Streetwalk & Walkways	OK	OK w/ Minor Work	Major Problems
Concrete cracked, eroded			
Tripping hazards			
Tree roots cracking, lifting slab			
Sections need repair			
Need to be completely replaced			
REMARKS			

Driveway			
Concrete cracked, eroded, damaged			
Blacktop cracked, worn, damaged			
Blacktop needs repair, recoating			
Concrete needs repair			
Needs to be completely replaced			
REMARKS			

Garage			
Number of outlets			
Settlement cracks in walls			
Concrete floor slab cracked			
Needs masonry work on walls			
Floor slab needs replacement			
Door needs refinishing			
Door needs replacement			
Door jambs rotted, need repair			
Door jambs need replacement			
Door hard to open, close			
Electric door opener needs repair			
REMARKS			

INTERIOR			
Foundation	OK	OK w/ Minor Work	**Major Problems**
Minor cracks			
Settlement cracks at corners, walls			
Wall bulging inward			
Seepage into basement/cellar			
Mortar deteriorating			
Needs complete rehabilitation			
REMARKS			
Basement or Cellar			
Number of outlets			
Seepage, water stains on floor			
Evidence of termites			
Sewage backing up, sump pump installed			
Waterproofing needed			
Old water main coming in			
Electrical ground not in place			
Shut-off, drain valves missing			
Handwheel malfunctions on shut-off valve			
Soil wet in crawl space			
Poor ventilation			
Need vapor barier in crawl space			
Debris needs to be cleared			
Space needs to be refinished			
Holes made in floor for termite treatment			
REMARKS			
Framing			
Need lally columns, concrete-filled			
Intermediate main beam missing			
Intermediate main beam rotted			

Framing, continued	OK	OK w/ Minor Work	Major Problems
Balloon- or platform-frame constructed			
Bracing or bridging required			
Sill plate damaged			
Evidence of termites			
Joists deflecting severely			
Joists undersized			
Joists sistered			
Subflooring damaged, loose			
Need subflooring			
REMARKS			
Kitchen			
Number of outlets			
Need ground-fault interrupter outlets			
Cracked walls, ceiling			
Loose plaster on walls, ceiling			
Loose nails, tape on drywall			
Soft, springy floor			
Wood, tiles on floor damaged			
Sink stained, cracked, chipped			
Faucet leaks			
Trap under sink leaks			
Shut-off valves in place under sink			
Water pressure and drainage checked			
Gurgling sound when sink drains			
Cabinets need refinishing			
Doors, drawers don't close			
Metal on cabinets rusted			
Hardware missing from cabinets			
Need new cabinets			
Counter top worn, stained			

Kitchen, continued	OK	OK w/ Minor Work	Major Problems
Need new counter top			
REMARKS			
Living Room			
Number of outlets			
Cracked walls, ceiling			
Loose plaster on walls, ceiling			
Loose nails, tape on drywall			
Soft, springy floors			
Wood or carpeting damaged			
Wood floor needs refinishing			
Carpeting needs replacement			
Water stains near windows			
REMARKS			
Dining Room			
Number of outlets			
Cracked walls, ceiling			
Loose plaster on walls, ceiling			
Loose nails, tape on drywall			
Soft, springy floors			
Wood or carpeting damaged			
Wood floor needs refinishing			
Carpeting needs replacement			
Water stains near windows			
REMARKS			
Porch			
Number of outlets			
Loose plaster on walls, ceiling			

Porch, continued	OK	OK w/ Minor Work	Major Problems
Loose nails, tape on drywall			
Soft, springy floors			
Wood or carpeting damaged			
Wood floor needs refinishing			
Carpeting needs replacement			
Water stains near windows			
REMARKS			
Staircase to Upper Level			
Damaged risers, treads			
Loose newel post, handrail			
Soft, springy treads			
Skirt board pulling away from wall			
Damaged carpeting			
Wood needs refinishing			
Need new carpeting			
Need to repair parts of staircase			
Need new staircase			
REMARKS			
Master Bedroom			
Number of outlets			
Cracked walls, ceiling			
Loose plaster on walls, ceiling			
Loose nails, tape on drywall			
Soft, springy floors			
Wood or carpeting damaged			
Wood floor needs refinishing			
Carpeting needs replacement			

Master Bedroom, continued	OK	OK w/ Minor Work	Major Problems
Water stains near windows			
REMARKS			
Bathroom Off Master Bedroom			
Number of outlets			
Need ground-fault interrupter outlets			
Cracked tiles, plaster on walls			
Cracked plaster on ceiling			
Loose tiles on walls, floor			
Loose nails, tape on drywall			
Damaged, missing tiles			
Wood floor rotted			
Soft, springy floor			
Wood floor needs refinishing			
Tile floor needs replacement			
Replaster, repaint ceiling			
Sink cracked, chipped, stained			
Gurgling sound when sink drains			
Water pressure and drainage checked			
Trap under sink leaks			
Shut-off valves in place under sink			
Faucet leaks			
Need new sink			
Toilet cracked, stained, chipped			
Water leaks at closet flange			
Need new toilet			
Tub cracked, stained, chipped			
Grout missing around tub			
Need new bathtub			
Shower pan damaged, leaks			
Shower door damaged, missing			
Water stains on ceiling below bathroom			

Bathroom Off Master Bedroom, continued	OK	OK w/ Minor Work	Major Problems
Need new shower			
Need new shower doors			
Need all new fixtures			
Need entirely new bathroom			
REMARKS			
Second Bathroom			
Number of outlets			
Cracked walls, ceiling			
Loose plaster on walls, ceiling			
Loose nails, tape on drywall			
Soft, springy floors			
Wood or carpeting damaged			
Wood floor needs refinishing			
Carpeting needs replacement			
Water stains near windows			
REMARKS			
Third Bedroom			
Number of outlets			
Cracked walls, ceiling			
Loose plaster on walls, ceiling			
Loose nails, tape on drywall			
Soft, springy floors			
Wood or carpeting damaged			
Wood floor needs refinishing			
Carpeting needs replacement			
Water stains near windows			
REMARKS			

Children's Bedroom	OK	OK w/ Minor Work	Major Problems
Number of outlets			
Cracked walls, ceiling			
Loose plaster on walls, ceiling			
Loose nails, tape on drywall			
Soft, springy floors			
Wood or carpeting damaged			
Wood floor needs refinishing			
Carpeting needs replacement			
Water stains near windows			
REMARKS			
Toilet Facility			
Number of outlets			
Need ground-fault interrupter outlets			
Cracked tiles, plaster on walls			
Cracked plaster on ceilings			
Loose tiles on walls, floor			
Loose nails, tape on drywall			
Damaged, missing tiles			
Wood floor rotted			
Soft, springy floor			
Wood floor needs refinishing			
Tile floor needs replacement			
Replaster, repaint ceiling			
Sink cracked, chipped, stained			
Gurgling sound when sink drains			
Water pressure and drainage checked			
Trap under sink leaks			
Shut-off valves in place under sink			
Faucet leaks			
Need new sink			
Toilet cracked, stained, chipped			

Toilet Facility, continued	OK	OK w/ Minor Work	Major Problems
Water leaks at closet flange			
Need new toilet			
Water stains on ceiling below this room			
Need entirely new toilet facility			
Need mechanical vent installed			
REMARKS			
Attic			
Needs ventilation such as vent windows			
Needs ridge vent, vented soffits			
Attic fan in place			
Insulation needed			
Number of vapor barriers			
Water entry from roof covering			
Damaged rafters, ridge board, fascia board			
Roof frame needs repair			
Stack vent ends in attic			
Soft, springy floor			
Needs to be heated			
Sheetrock® walls damaged			
Insulation blocking air circulation			
May be old asbestos insulation			
Access to attic needs repair			
Stairs to attic need replacement			
Collar beam in place			
Collar beam damaged			
REMARKS			
Cock Loft (house with flat roof)			
Hatch in place, closes securely			
Needs roof vent			

Cock Loft, continued	OK	OK w/ Minor Work	Major Problems
Evidence of water entry			
Damaged roof rafters			
Needs insulation			
REMARKS			

SYSTEMS

Plumbing			
Old galvanized piping in place			
Copper or brass piping in place			
Dissimilar materials being used			
Pipe insulation crumbling, missing			
Pipe insulation may be asbestos			
Need to insulate pipes			
Pipes leaking			
Leaks, corrosion on drain lines			
Drain lines need replacement			
REMARKS			

Electrical Service			
Need more service in house			
Old fuse box in place			
Need new circuit breaker panel box			
Need more circuit breakers			
Aluminum wiring in use			
Pull-chain switches in use			
Outlets, switches damaged			
Old wiring still in use			
Outlets not grounded in use			
Need grounded outlets installed			
Extension cords in use			

Electrical Service, continued	OK	OK w/ Minor Work	Major Problems
Need more outlets installed			
Ground-fault interrupter outlets needed			
Underground service feed in place			
Overhead service feed in place			
Trees could damage overhead service feed			
REMARKS			

Heating System			
Boiler gas, oil-fired			
Electrically-fired furnace			
Boiler is old, converted from coal to oil			
Boiler not serviced frequently			
Evidence of water leakage around boiler			
Thermostat turns on boiler			
Emergency and shut-off switches turn off boiler			
Boiler needs cleaning			
Chimney flue needs cleaning, repair			
Metal flue pipe patched, needs replacement			
Boiler needs replacement			
Fire brick needs rehabilitation			
Forced-air furnace noisy			
Flame not centered in heat exchanger			
Draft is poor in heat exchanger			
Furnace needs cleaning, adjustment			
Coil to heat water corroded			
Need new coil or hot water heater			
Pressure safety valve in place			
REMARKS			

Domestic Hot Water Heater	OK	OK w/ Minor Work	Major Problems
Needs greater capacity			
Tank corroded			
Water stains on floor			
Leaks at inlet and outlet connections			
Pressure safety valve in place			
Metal flue pipe patched, needs replacement			
Heater not serviced frequently			
Short life expectancy			
Tank needs replacement			
Burner marks at lighting panel			
Flexible connector in place must be changed			
REMARKS			

Comparing Features in . . .	House #1	House #2	House #3
Exterior			
Siding or shingles well maintained			
Brick or stucco well maintained			
Roof covering new or in good shape			
Parapet wall in good condition			
Gutters, leaders new or in good shape			
Doors new and energy-efficient			
Windows new and energy-efficient			
Chimney in good condition			
Front entrance steps in good shape			
Side or back steps in good shape			
Streetwalk in good condition			
Walkways in good condition			
Driveway in good condition			
Garage in good shape			
Garage roof new or in good shape			
Landscaping attractive and neat			
Interior			
Concrete foundation sound			
Block foundation sound			
Brick foundation sound			
Foundation's footings not damaged			
Finished basement			
Insect infestation, wood decay not found			
Framing in good condition			
Large, modern kitchen			
House has largest number of rooms			
House has largest number of bedrooms			
House has largest number of bathrooms			
Bathrooms modern, new fixtures			
Interior rooms spacious, in good shape			
Finished attic			
Attic well-insulated			

Comparing Features in . . .	House #1	House #2	House #3
Systems			
Brass or copper plumbing in use			
Drain lines cast-iron or galvanized			
Water main is copper			
Electrical system updated and grounded			
Aluminum wiring not in use			
Heating system new and energy-efficient			
Domestic hot water heater in use			
Asbestos not being used as insulation			
Extra Features			
Central air conditioning			
Fireplaces in use are clean and lined			
Pool			
Deck			
Patio			
Greenhouse/sunroom			
Conclusions			
No code violations			
Little minor work has to be done			
No major problems have to be resolved			
Summary			
House has the most marks in this checklist			
Type of professional advice needed			
Cost of resolving any problems			
House most favored in this checklist			

Glossary

ABSTRACT (OF TITLE) — Set of public records that are related to the title of a piece of land. Usually a title company or attorney reviews these records to check for, and clear away, any discrepancies before buyer can purchase property.

AGREEMENT OF SALE — Called a contract. This contract is an agreement between seller and buyer for selling and purchasing a piece of property.

AIR DUCT — Rectangular or round metal pipe used to convey warm or cold air through house and back to forced-air furnace, or to air conditioning unit.

ALLIGATORING — Open cracks or fissures in the surface of a paint coating. This criss-cross pattern is caused by expansion or contraction of new top coat over a slippery undercoat.

AMPERE — The unit of currents. This current flows through a conductor. It is produced flowing through a conductor whose resistance is one ohm. The conductor has a potential difference of one volt between its ends.

ANCHOR BOLT — Threaded steel bolt used to secure wood sill plate to foundation wall.

APPRAISAL — An individual's judgment of the value of the piece of property.

ASPHALT — Black bituminous coating used for blacktop for driveways, in roof coverings, and in wall shingles.

BACKFILL — Earth is replaced and tamped down around foundation walls, after work on and around foundation walls has been completed.

BALLOON-FRAMING — Old type of framing using long wall studs which are secured to sill plate. After studs are secured, floor joists are secured to them.

BALUSTERS — Spindles of upright members attached to handrail and stair treads.

BALUSTRADE — Handrail used at end of stairs and on landings.

BEAM — Horizontal structural member which can be steel or wood (main support timber). Used to support floor joists and partitions.

BEARING WALL — Wall supporting roof load or floor load, depending upon its placement. There may be a bearing wall on each floor of a building.

BEVEL SIDING — Wood siding attached to exterior walls with nails. Looks wedge-shaped in cross-section.

BINDER — Agreement between buyer and seller in which buyer agrees to pay a fixed amount of money to secure his/her right to purchase property.

BLEACHING OIL — Oil stain used on wood siding, decking, etc., to accelerate the weathering process.

BLISTERS — Soft raised or puffed spots appearing on siding where paint was improperly applied. Also may be seen on roof covering that was improperly installed.

BRACE — A piece of framing member or wood subfloor installed at an angle or incline to stiffen the structural members.

BRICK VENEER — A brick facing applied to wood-framed house. It is attached to sheathing of framed walls with metal ties.

BRIDGING — Metal member or short length of wood member used between floor joists in a diagonal position to brace and stiffen joists and to distribute loading.

BUILDING CODE — Legal codes required by town, city, state for the design, construction of residential and commercial buildings. Written to protect people who live and/or work in these buildings.

BUILDING LINE — Distance from the sides, front, and back of a lot beyond which a building cannot extend, depending upon local code.

CASEMENT — A window sash supported by hinges which open and close the sash. Hinges are fastened to one side of the vertical frame.

CASING — Window and door framing.

CAVITY WALL — A hollow wall section created by wood framing members and usually insulated.

CERTIFICATE OF TITLE — Issued by a title company. Indicates that the seller has good marketable and insurable title to the property he/she is offering for sale.

CHIMNEY CAP — A concrete cover at the top of a brick chimney.

CIRCUIT BREAKER — An electric safety device housed in an electrical box which breaks an electric circuit automatically when it becomes overloaded. Breaker moves from "On" to "Off" position.

CLAPBOARD — Wood exterior siding that is thicker on one edge than the other. Comes in a variety of lengths. It is overlapped and nailed into sheathing.

CLOSING COSTS — A number of expenses associated with completing the transaction in the transfer of ownership of real estate including attorney's fee, partial heating, electric, and tax bills, etc.

CLOSING DAY — Day on which seller and buyer meet to conclude formalities of real estate sale.

COCK LOFT — Small space between top floor ceiling and roof.

COMMISSION — Money paid to real estate broker by the seller for facilitating the sale of the property.

COLLAR BEAM — Wood beam connecting two inclined roof rafters. It helps to stiffen the framing of a pitched roof structure.

COLUMN — A vertical member such as a lally column used to support main beams, roofs, etc.

COPING — A tile cap used to cover the top of a parapet wall or any regular masonry wall.

CONCRETE — A mixture of Portland cement, sand, gravel, and water used in building construction for foundation walls, floor slabs, footings, etc.

CONDENSATION — Drops of water formed when warm moist air is put in contact with an area having a lower temperature than that air. Drops form when air can no longer hold moisture.

CONDUCTOR — Material used to transmit an electric current, such as copper wire.

CONDUIT — A metal pipe used to carry electric wire throughout the inside and outside of a house.

CORNICE — Wood or metal decorative projection at the roof level of a building. It usually projects outward and is located at the front of the building.

COUNTER FLASHING — Sheet metal placed at the base of a parapet wall over the roof covering, or at the base of a chimney, to prevent water entry.

CRAWL SPACE — A narrow, unfinished area usually filled with soil located in the cellar or basement.

CRIPPLE STUDS — Short wood members used above and below window and door openings to support frame.

DECAY — Disintegration of wood fibers by action due to insects, wood-decaying fungus, or water damage.

DEED — A written document through which title to the property being sold is transferred.

DEHUMIDIFIER — A device that removes moisture from the air.

DEPRECIATION — Decline in the price of a piece of property due to economic trends, wear and tear of the property, and popularity of the location of the property such as proximity to beach that is eroding.

DOOR JAMB — Wood casing surrounding a door. Door opens and closes into this jamb.

DOUBLE-GLAZED — Insulating glass which is constructed of two panes of glass with a sealed air space between them.

DOUBLE-HUNG WINDOW — Window with a top and bottom sash raised and lowered by weights attached to cords or chains.

DOWN PAYMENT — Amount of money the seller receives upon signing an agreement to sell his/her property with balance to be paid later.

DRYWALL — A type of interior wall construction applied in 4′ × 8′ sheets, often called by the trade name Sheetrock®.

EASEMENT RIGHTS — Permission of right-of-way granted to a person or company giving access to or across the owner's land.

EAVES — The projection of the roof beyond the house's walls.

EFFLORESCENCE — Water stains formed on the surface of brick or concrete caused by moisture penetration.

ENCROACHMENT — A building that extends beyond its building line or projects onto another individual's property.

ENCUMBRANCE — A claim against property that diminishes that property's value.

EQUITY — The market value of the property minus any loans, liens, or debts against that property.

ESCROW — Funds held in reserve until a specified event has been completed.

EXPANSION JOINT — Bituminous fiber strip used to divide sections of concrete streetwalk or blocks to prevent cracking due to expansion.

FASCIA — Flat wood member covering a section of eave or cornice. The roof gutter is supported by this fascia.

FILL-TYPE INSULATION — Loose material used for insulating wall cavities, such as rock wool or cellulose.

FIRE BOX — An area of combustion in the boiler.

FIRE BRICK — Bricks used to line the interior of the fire box chamber.

FIRE-STOP — Usually 2 × 4 wood blocking put between studs in a partition wall to prevent the spread of fire and smoke.

FLASHING — Sheet metal used at wall and roof junctions and at chimney and roof junctions to prevent water entry.

FLOOR JOISTS — Framing members which span from one foundation wall to the other side of foundation wall, or sometimes rest on intermediate main beams.

FLUE — An air channel, usually a pipe, in a chimney, which allows smoke and fumes of combustion to exit into the air.

FLUE LINER — Terra cotta tile or fire clay material, round or square, used as a lining inside brick chimney of heating system or fireplace. Usually available in 2′-long sections.

FLUE PIPE — Metal cylindrical pipe used to allow smoke and products of combustion from furnace, boiler, or hot water heater to exhaust into chimney and out of house.

FOOTING — A section of concrete that the house's foundation walls sit on.

FOUNDATION — A block, brick, stone, or concrete wall on which the house's framing is built. It is mostly below grade.

FORECLOSURE — Bank or mortgage lender assumes ownership of property due to failure to pay loan.

FRAMING — Construction lumber used to form structure such as floor joists, floor rafters, wall studs, etc.

FROST LINE — The depth to which frost can penetrate the soil. Footings should be placed below frost line.

FUNGUS — Plants that live in wood and cause it to decay and be stained. Also can be found in wood in damp areas in house such as in crawl space.

FUSE — Small, screw-type safety device used in an electric panel box to break circuit when it becomes overloaded.

GABLE — Steep triangular roof shape in which rafters are attached from ridge board to double top plate. A house with a gable roof usually has a spacious attic.

GRADE LINE — The location where the soil rests against the foundation wall.

GRADE STAMP — Stamped marking on lumber indicating quality, type of wood, if kiln-dry. For example, No. 1, K.D., Hem-Fir.

GRANTEE — The person/persons on the deed who is/are buying the property.

GRANTOR — The person/persons on the deed who is/are selling the property.

GUTTER — A metal or wood channel supported at the eave to convey rainwater away from the structure.

HEADER — A framing member that sits on the sill plate and to which floor joists are attached.

HUMIDIFIER — A device used to increase or maintain relative moisture in the air in a house or room.

INSULATION — Material used to resist loss of heat energy and to reduce the transfer of sound or electricity.

INTEREST — A charge (amount of money) paid for the loan of money.

JAMB — Wood or metal casing surrounding a door or window.

JOIST — A series of rectangular sections, usually wooden, used to support floor and ceiling loads.

KILN-DRY — Lumber that has been dried in a kiln with the use of heat to a moisture content of six to twelve percent.

KNEE WALL — Framing member used for wall construction in an attic.

LALLY COLUMN — A round steel pillar used to support a beam or joist. Usually it is concrete-filled.

LEADER — A metal downspout connected to the gutter to convey rainwater away from property.

LIEN — A claim made by an individual on another individual's property to pay for money owed.

LINTEL — A horizontal structural member, usually made of steel or sometimes stone, used to support the area of the wall above a window or door opening.

LOAD-BEARING WALL — Same as bearing wall. Used to support roof or floor load.

MASONRY — Walls constructed of brick, block, stone, etc.

MOISTURE BARRIER — Treated paper or foil used to keep moisture from moving from one area to another. Paper or foil is on the back of roll-type insulation and foil is on insulation board.

MORTGAGE — A loan from the lender to the buyer against the property.

MORTGAGE COMMITMENT — Notice from a bank or lending institution saying it is advancing mortgage funds.

MORTGAGE NOTE — An agreement in writing to repay the loan by the borrower.

MORTGAGE (OPEN-END) — Gives permission to borrow additional money in the future without refinancing the loan.

MORTGAGEE — Person or institution that holds the mortgage.

MORTGAGOR — The borrower.

NEWEL POST — The main post at the foot of the staircase. The balustrade (handrail) is attached to the newel post.

NON-BEARING WALL — Wall that supports only its weight and does not support a load from the roof, floor, etc.

NOSING — Rounded edge of a stair tread that projects over a stair riser.

ON CENTER — The measure for the spacing between floor joists, wall studs, etc. For instance, 16″ on center means that the studs are spaced 16″ apart from the center of each stud.

PARTITION — An interior wall which divides a space such as one that separates one room from another.

PITCH — The slope or incline of a roof.

PLASTER — Mixture of lime, sand, and water used mostly to cover interior wall and ceiling surfaces.

PLATFORM-FRAMING — A system of framing of a structure in which the wall studs are attached to the sole plate and top plate. This wall section is attached to the subfloor and floor joists. Each stud wall is only one story high.

POINTS — Additional charges placed on borrowed money for a mortgage, usually levied when money is tight.

POINTING — Repair of joints in brick or block construction done by refilling joints with mortar.

POST & BEAM CONSTRUCTION — A system of construction in which beams (timbers) are supported by heavy posts instead of joists and studs.

PORCH — An area extending beyond the exterior walls of a house which can be enclosed or left open.

PREPAYMENT — Payment of a mortgage loan, or of part of it, before it becomes due for payment.

PRINCIPAL — That portion of a loan which is not the interest on that mortgage loan.

PUTTY — A soft, pliable compound used for sealing glass in a sash or for repairing small holes.

R VALUE — Resistance to heat transfer of material.

RADIANT FLOOR HEATING — Tubing with hot water flowing in it embedded in concrete floor, or installed under wood floor, used to heat a room.

RAFTER — Structural member used to frame and support roof. It spans from exterior wall to ridge board.

REAL ESTATE BROKER — An individual who assists a property owner in finding a buyer for his/her property.

REFINANCING — Obtaining a second loan to assist in paying off the first loan.

REINFORCED CONCRETE — Concrete with steel rods or wire embedded to give the concrete mixture extra strength.

RIDGE BOARD — Board placed at peak of roof to support one end of roof rafters. Other end of roof rafter is attached to double top plate.

RISER — The vertical section of a step in a staircase.

ROCK WOOL — An insulating material similar to fiberglass which can be blown into wall cavities. It has a high melting point.

ROLL ROOFING PAPER — Roofing material (felt) made with asphalt fibers. Heaviest weight is 10-lb. and roll is 36″ wide.

ROOF — The covering on top of a building.

ROOF SHEATHING — Plywood or similar sheets which are fastened to the roof rafters. Building paper is applied and then roof covering.

SAG — A dip or deflection in a joist, or an unevenness in a coat of paint.

SASH — The window frame that houses the glass pane.

SATURATED FELT — Roll roofing paper that has been saturated with asphalt.

SEEPAGE PIT — A septic tank and cesspool making up a system for sewage disposal.

SEPTIC TANK — A tank in which sewage settles to the bottom where part of it is destroyed by bacteria and the rest is discharged to a leaching bed.

SHAKES — Wood shingles that have been hand-cut.

SHEATHING — Plywood or similar sheets, usually 4′ × 8′, which are nailed onto exterior studding and rafters and covered with roof covering or exterior siding.

SHINGLES — A siding or roof covering applied in overlapping layers, usually made of asphalt, wood, asbestos, slate, etc.

SIDING — Wood boards or metal sections nailed vertically or horizontally to sheathing. The siding may be overlapped if installed horizontally, or it may interlock vertically as with metal siding.

SILL PLATE — Wood member that rests on foundation wall and is attached to it with anchor bolts. Floor joists and header are attached to it.

SKIRT BOARD — A horizontal member attached to wall studs at an incline to support a staircase's treads and risers.

SLAB — A concrete floor poured directly onto the soil which may have a bed of gravel in it or reinforcing steel bars criss-crossed in it.

SOFFIT — Underside of the eave or cornice.

SOLE PLATE — The bottom wood member of a framed stud wall.

SOLID BRIDGING — A short wood member placed between the floor joists at the center to prevent the joists from twisting.

SPALLING — Hard outer surface of brick separates and falls off exposing brick's soft interior. This occurs when water freezes and expands after it has penetrated a porous or cracked brick wall, forcing the brick's surface to pull away. Exposure of the brick's soft interior accelerates the deterioration of the brick.

SPECIAL ASSESSMENT — A tax added onto a piece of property to cover costs for road construction, sewers, sidewalks, etc.

SPLASH BLOCK — A masonry section placed under leader pipe to divert water drainage away from the foundation of a house.

STRINGER — A long wood member placed at an incline as a sidewall to support a staircase.

STUD — Wood member used for wall framing, usually 16″ on center.

SUBFLOOR — Plywood or similar wood sheet nailed to floor joists on which finished flooring is installed.

SUSPENDED CEILING — Fabricated tiles supported by a metal grid hung from the old ceiling and by wall angles attached to the walls.

SUMP — Pit in basement housing house trap and water main. Sump pump often found installed in this pit to pump out any water that collects in pit.

TAX — A charge on income and real estate to be used for services provided by town, county, city, state, or federal government.

TERMITES — Insects that live in and destroy wood. They resemble ants and destroy the wood framing in a house.

TERMITE SHIELD — A piece of metal attached to a foundation wall to serve as a barrier against termites.

TIE — A wood member that holds a pair of rafters at or near the bottom for support.

TITLE — A document that states ownership or possession of a piece of property.

TITLE INSURANCE — Protection against loss of interest for the lender or homeowner in case of a defect in the title.

TITLE SEARCH — An investigation of the property about to be purchased to make sure that there are no liens or loans on it, that the owner is properly entitled to sell the house, etc.

TOP PLATE — Wood members, usually known as a double top plate, that form the top of a framed wall. The roof rafters and ceiling joists are supported by the top plate.

TREAD — The horizontal part of the staircase on which a person steps to ascend or descend the stairs.

TRAP — Usually a 4″ diameter cast-iron pipe, called the house trap, with a U bend which acts as a seal as water passes through it. It prevents sewer gases from entering into a house.

TRUSS — An assembly often used in roof construction composed of roof rafters, horizontal joists, and braces.

U VALUE — Heat transfer coefficient of material.

VALLEY — Angle formed at the intersection of two sections of sloped roofs.

VAPOR BARRIER — Material used to prevent passage of vapor or moisture from one area to another. Kraft paper or foil is used on roll-type (batt) insulation, foil used on insulation board. Sometimes a plastic membrane is installed over insulation without a vapor barrier before the inside walls are covered.

VENT STACK — A pipe riser that extends through the roof to the outside atmosphere to allow sewer gases to escape from plumbing system.

VERMICULITE — Bulk insulation material similar to mica.

VOLT — A unit of electrical potential difference and electromotive force.

WALL SHEATHING — Plywood sheets, usually 4' × 8', which are nailed to wall studs on outside. Exterior siding is applied over wall sheathing.

WATT — An electrical unit of power equal to one ampere running through a conductor with one volt of force.

WEATHERING — Discoloration of wood surface due to prolonged exposure to sun, rain, wind, light, etc. Application of a bleaching oil will speed up this process.

WEEP HOLE — Small hole in masonry wall that permits water to drain from behind wall.

ZONING ORDINANCE — Code defined by town, county, city, or other locality to govern building and land uses.

Bibliography

A Citizen's Guide to Radon. U.S. Environmental Protection Agency, August 1986.

Adelman, Dennis. "Radiant Floor Heating." *Fine Homebuilding.* The Taunton Press, Newtown, CT, August/September 1984, Volume #22.

Exposed Cedar. Western Wood Products Association, Portland, OR, December 1988.

Feirer, John L. and Gilbert R. Hutchings. *Carpentry and Building Construction.* Charles Scribner's Sons, New York, 1976.

Lead and Your Drinking Water. U.S. Environmental Protection Agency, April 1987.

Luttrell, Michael. "Warm Floors." *Fine Homebuilding.* The Taunton Press, Newtown, CT, June/July 1985, Volume #27.

Marks, Lionel S. *Mechanical Engineering Handbook.* McGraw-Hill Book Company, New York and London.

Redwood Exterior Guide. California Redwood Association, One Lombard St., San Francisco, CA 94111.

Roofing & Insulation. Johns-Manville Corp., P.O. Box 5108, Denver, CO 80217.

Subterranean Termites. U.S. Department of Agriculture Forest Service, Home and Garden Bulletin #64, October 1983.

Termiticides. U.S. Environmental Protection Agency, February 1988.

Wood Decay in Houses. U.S. Department of Agriculture Forest Service, Home and Garden Bulletin #73, August 1977.

You Can Protect Your Home From Termites. U.S. Department of Agriculture Forest Service.

*Available from the Superintendent of Documents, U.S. Government Printing Office, Washington, DC 20402.

Other information available from:

American Society of Heating, Refrigeration and Air-Conditioning Engineers, 1791 Tullie Circle, N.E., Atlanta, GA 30329.

American Wood Preservers Institute, 1651 Old Meadow Rd., McLean, VA 22101.

Western Wood Products Association, Yeon Building, 522 SW Fifth Ave., Portland, OR 97204.

SCHEMATIC OF ONE-PIPE STEAM SYSTEM

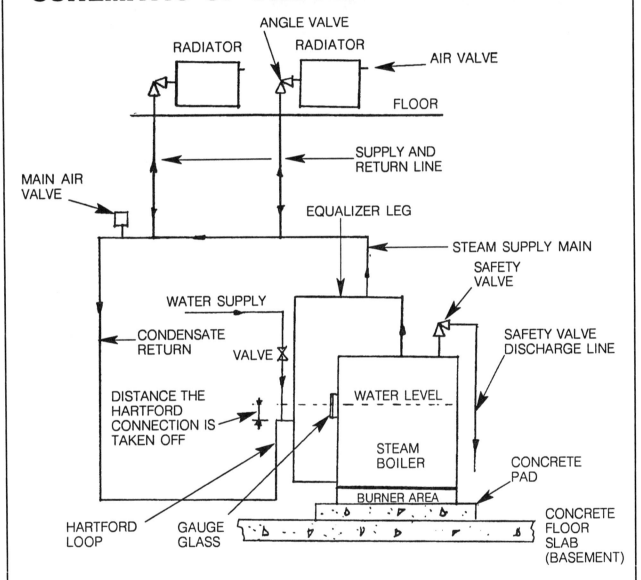

NOTE: THE HARTFORD LOOP PREVENTS TOO MUCH LOSS OF WATER
FROM THE BOILER IN CASE OF A FAILURE IN THE RETURN LINE.

SCHEMATIC OF TWO-PIPE HOT WATER SYSTEM

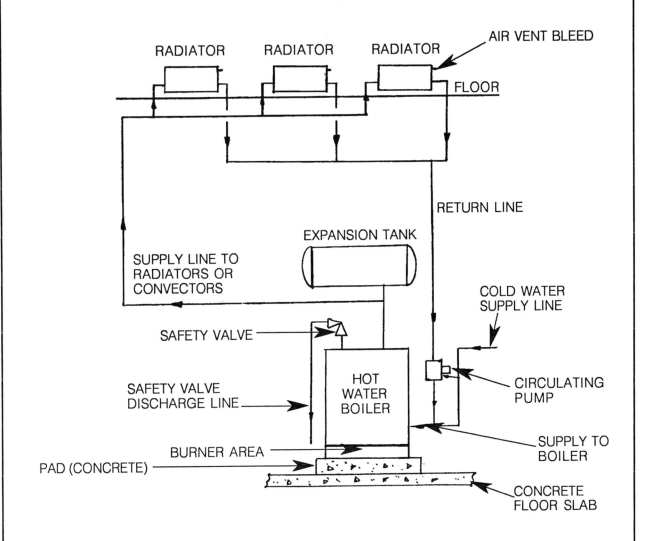

NOTE: EXPANSION TANK IS USED FOR EXPANSION AND CONTRACTION OF WATER. WITH THE RISE IN TEMPERATURE, WATER WILL EXPAND, AND ADDITIONAL VOLUME WILL FLOW INTO THE EXPANSION TANK.

ILLUSTRATION C ▪ 101

SCHEMATIC OF FORCED-AIR SYSTEM

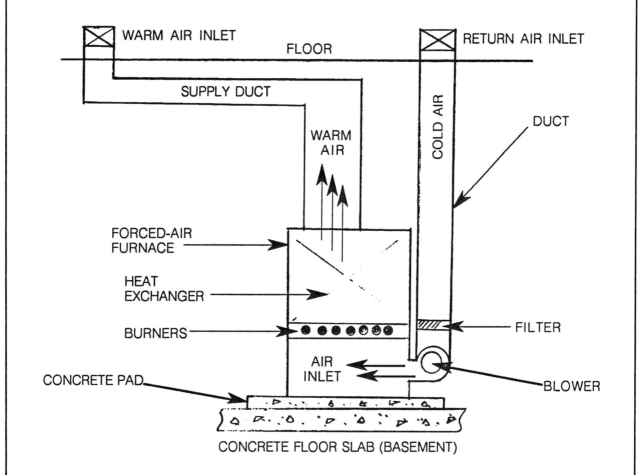

SCHEMATIC OF FORCEMAIN SYSTEM

TYPICAL ARRANGEMENT OF FORCED-AIR SYSTEM USED FOR CENTRAL AIR CONDITIONING

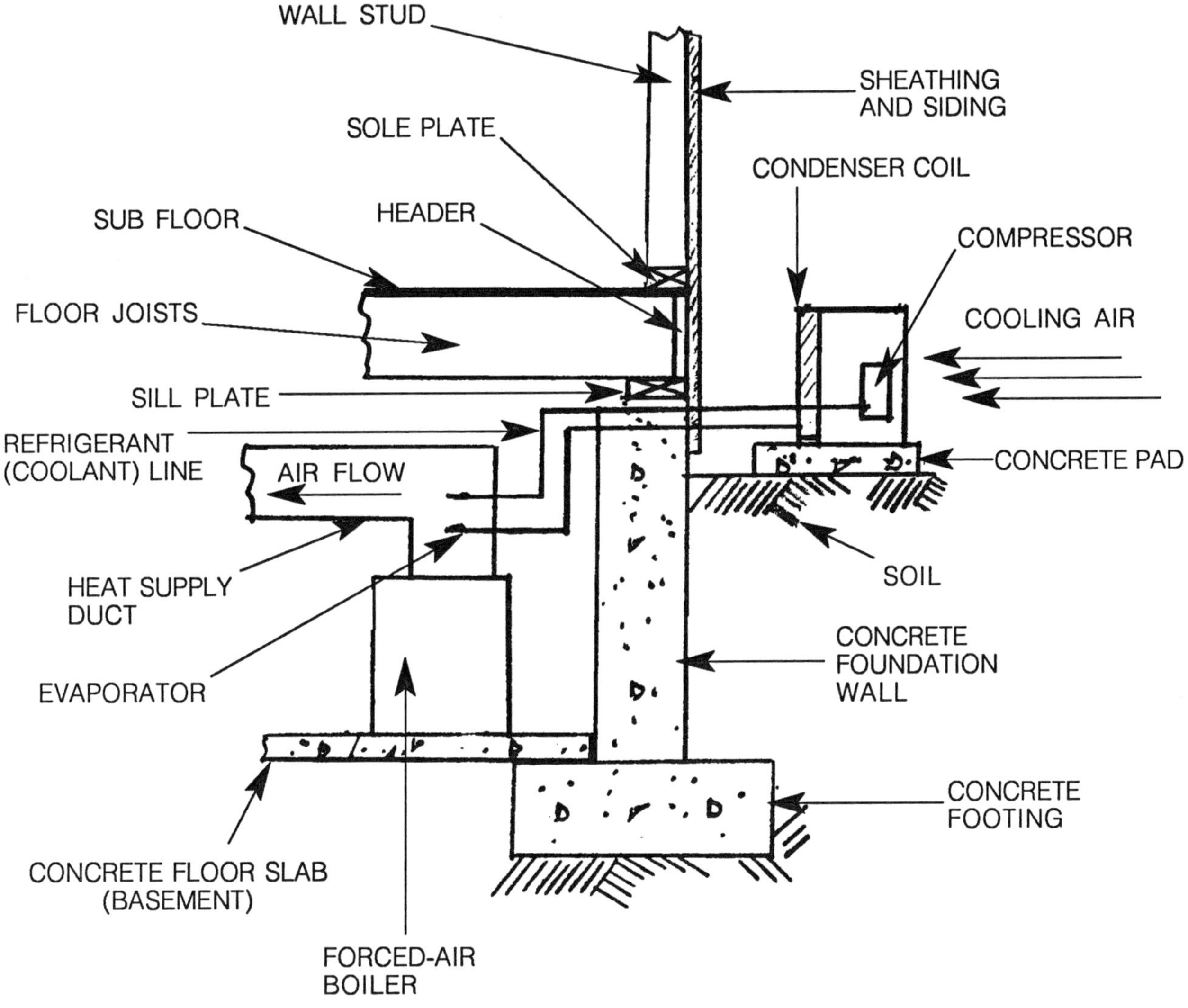

WALL STUD

SHEATHING AND SIDING

SOLE PLATE

CONDENSER COIL

SUB FLOOR

HEADER

COMPRESSOR

FLOOR JOISTS

COOLING AIR

SILL PLATE

REFRIGERANT (COOLANT) LINE

AIR FLOW

CONCRETE PAD

HEAT SUPPLY DUCT

SOIL

EVAPORATOR

CONCRETE FOUNDATION WALL

CONCRETE FLOOR SLAB (BASEMENT)

CONCRETE FOOTING

FORCED-AIR BOILER

GAS AND ELECTRIC HOT WATER HEATERS

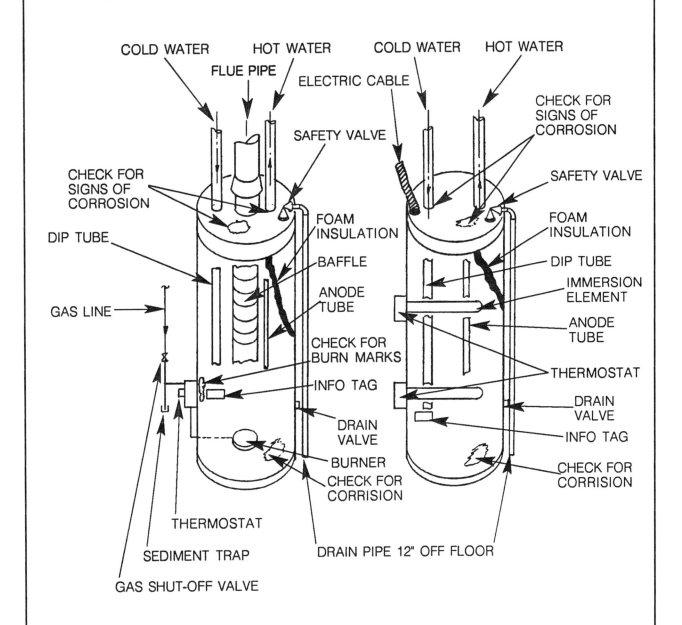

GAS WATER HEATER

ELECTRIC WATER HEATER

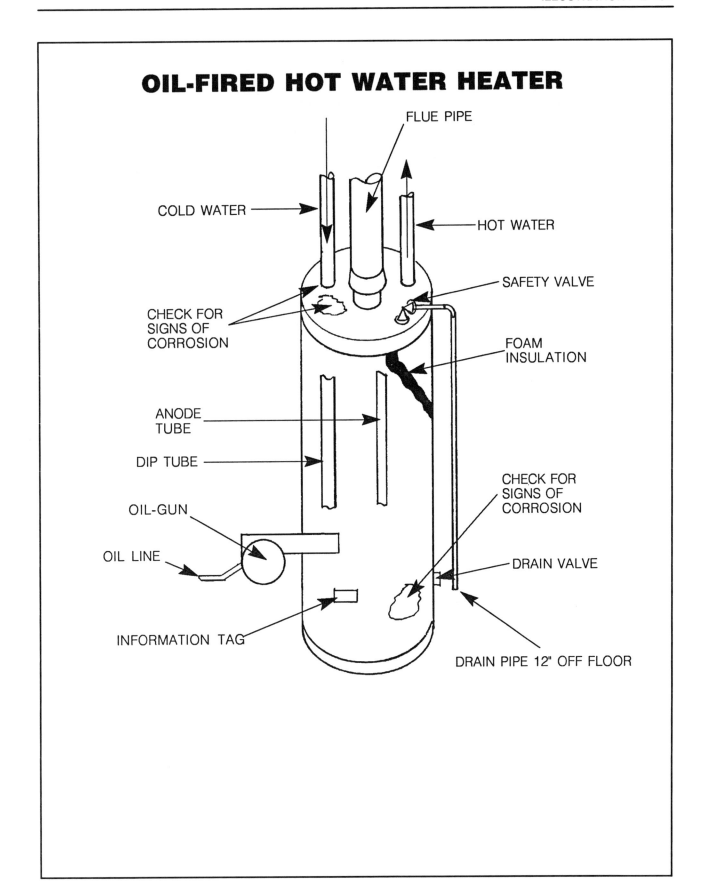

OIL-FIRED HOT WATER HEATER

SECTION OF MAIN CIRCUIT BREAKER BOX

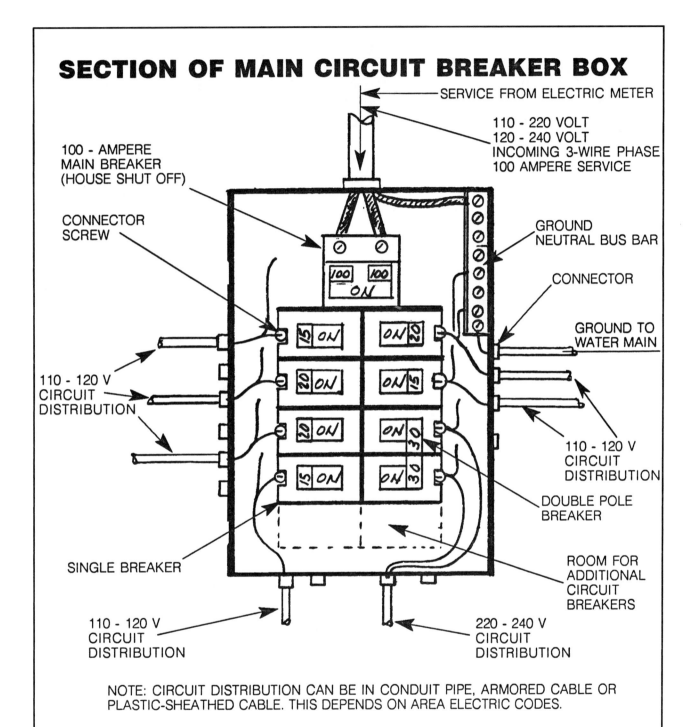

SERVICE FROM ELECTRIC METER

110 - 220 VOLT
120 - 240 VOLT
INCOMING 3-WIRE PHASE
100 AMPERE SERVICE

100 - AMPERE
MAIN BREAKER
(HOUSE SHUT OFF)

CONNECTOR
SCREW

GROUND
NEUTRAL BUS BAR

CONNECTOR

GROUND TO
WATER MAIN

110 - 120 V
CIRCUIT
DISTRIBUTION

110 - 120 V
CIRCUIT
DISTRIBUTION

DOUBLE POLE
BREAKER

SINGLE BREAKER

ROOM FOR
ADDITIONAL
CIRCUIT
BREAKERS

110 - 120 V
CIRCUIT
DISTRIBUTION

220 - 240 V
CIRCUIT
DISTRIBUTION

NOTE: CIRCUIT DISTRIBUTION CAN BE IN CONDUIT PIPE, ARMORED CABLE OR PLASTIC-SHEATHED CABLE. THIS DEPENDS ON AREA ELECTRIC CODES.

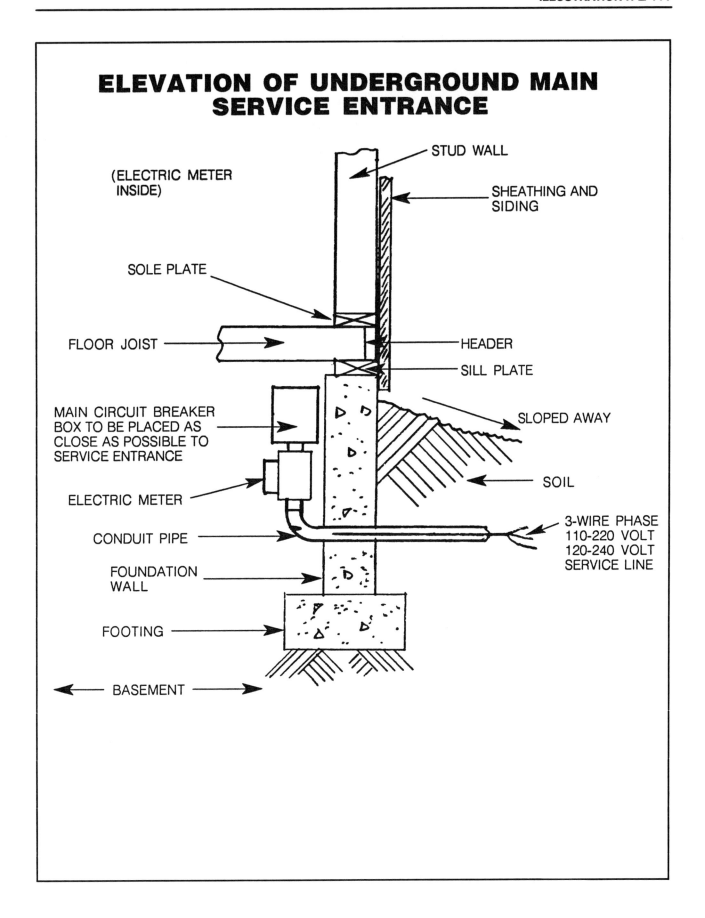

ELEVATION OF UNDERGROUND MAIN SERVICE ENTRANCE

ILLUSTRATION I ■ 113

ELEVATION OF OVERHEAD MAIN SERVICE ENTRANCE (ELECTRIC METER OUTSIDE)

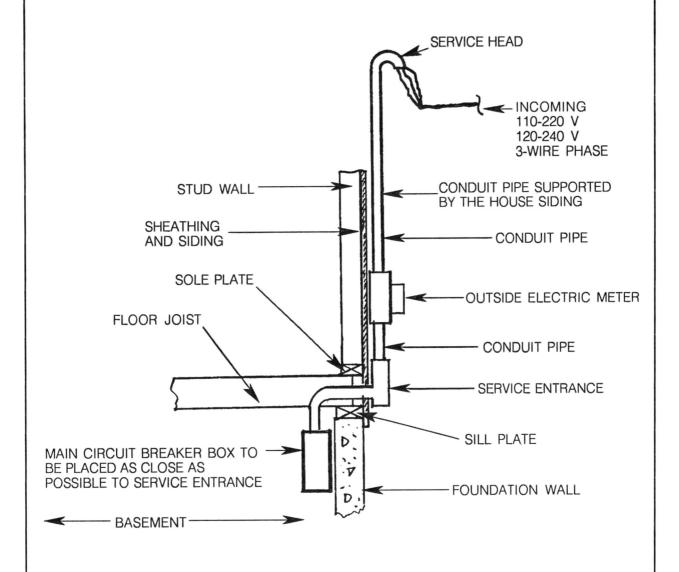

TYPICAL SEWER AND WATER LINE ARRANGEMENT

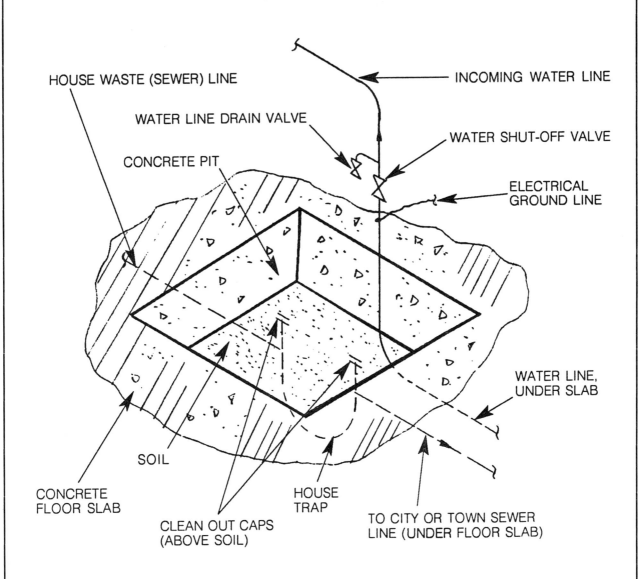

HOUSE WASTE (SEWER) LINE

WATER LINE DRAIN VALVE

CONCRETE PIT

INCOMING WATER LINE

WATER SHUT-OFF VALVE

ELECTRICAL GROUND LINE

WATER LINE, UNDER SLAB

SOIL

CONCRETE FLOOR SLAB

CLEAN OUT CAPS (ABOVE SOIL)

HOUSE TRAP

TO CITY OR TOWN SEWER LINE (UNDER FLOOR SLAB)

NOTE: CHECK SOIL FOR EVIDENCE OF SEWER LINE BACKUP

SCHEMATIC PLUMBING LAYOUT

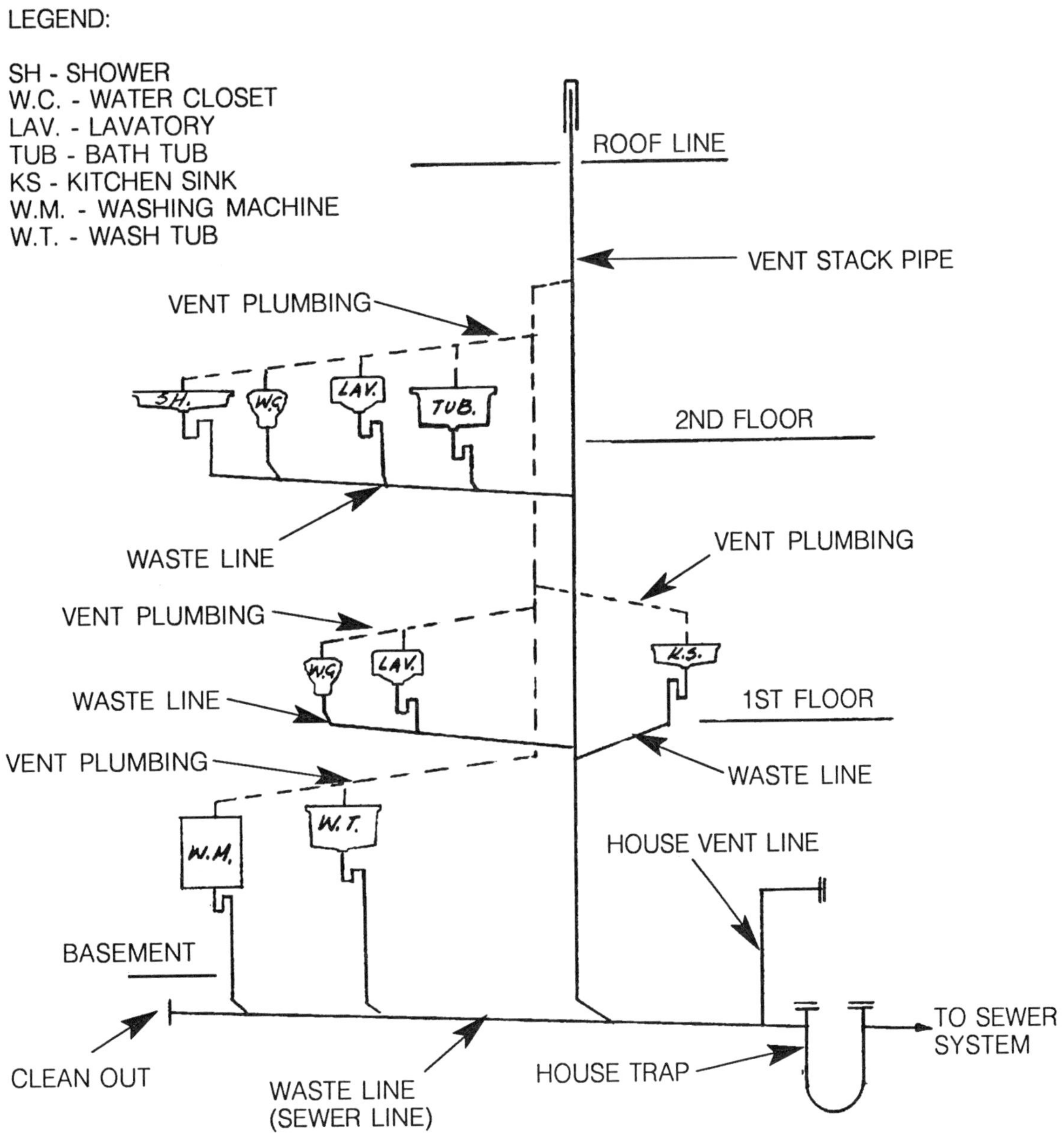

LEGEND:

SH - SHOWER
W.C. - WATER CLOSET
LAV. - LAVATORY
TUB - BATH TUB
KS - KITCHEN SINK
W.M. - WASHING MACHINE
W.T. - WASH TUB

ROOF LINE

VENT STACK PIPE

VENT PLUMBING

SH. | WC | LAV. | TUB.

2ND FLOOR

WASTE LINE

VENT PLUMBING

VENT PLUMBING

WC | LAV.

K.S.

WASTE LINE

1ST FLOOR

VENT PLUMBING

WASTE LINE

W.M. | W.T.

HOUSE VENT LINE

BASEMENT

TO SEWER SYSTEM

CLEAN OUT

WASTE LINE
(SEWER LINE)

HOUSE TRAP

ILLUSTRATION L ■ 119

TYPICAL ROOF FRAMING, COVERING AND GUTTER, LEADER DETAIL

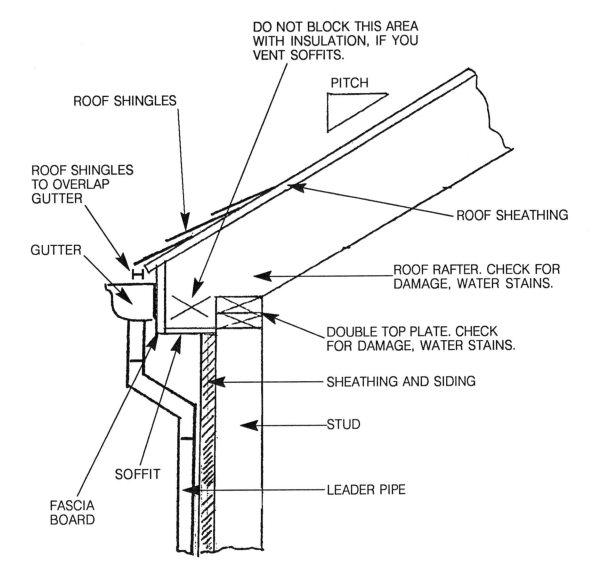

DO NOT BLOCK THIS AREA WITH INSULATION, IF YOU VENT SOFFITS.

PITCH

ROOF SHINGLES

ROOF SHINGLES TO OVERLAP GUTTER

ROOF SHEATHING

GUTTER

ROOF RAFTER. CHECK FOR DAMAGE, WATER STAINS.

DOUBLE TOP PLATE. CHECK FOR DAMAGE, WATER STAINS.

SHEATHING AND SIDING

STUD

SOFFIT

LEADER PIPE

FASCIA BOARD

FLAT ROOF, PARAPET WALL, AND COCK LOFT

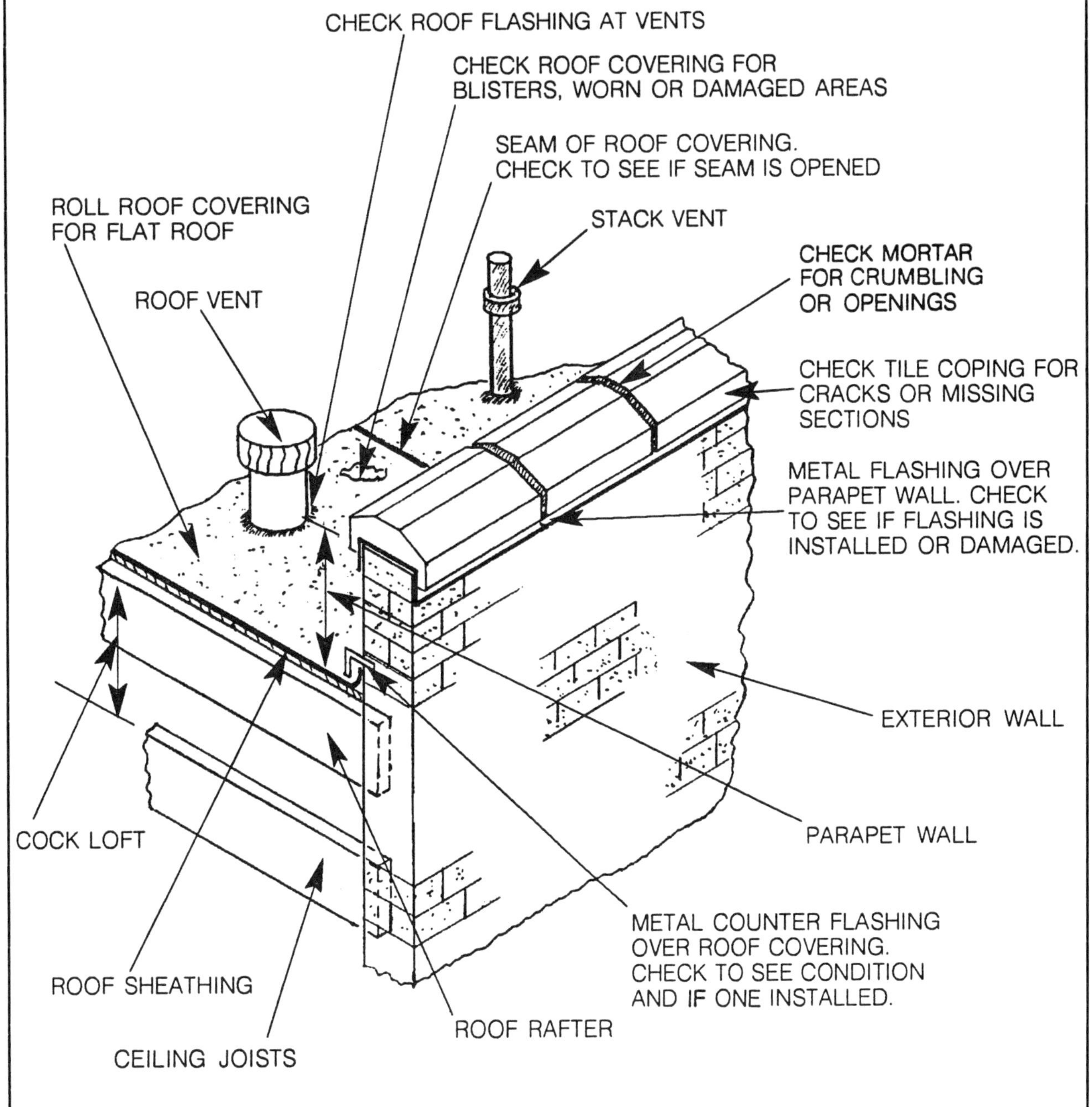

CHECK ROOF FLASHING AT VENTS

CHECK ROOF COVERING FOR
BLISTERS, WORN OR DAMAGED AREAS

SEAM OF ROOF COVERING.
CHECK TO SEE IF SEAM IS OPENED

STACK VENT

CHECK MORTAR
FOR CRUMBLING
OR OPENINGS

CHECK TILE COPING FOR
CRACKS OR MISSING
SECTIONS

METAL FLASHING OVER
PARAPET WALL. CHECK
TO SEE IF FLASHING IS
INSTALLED OR DAMAGED.

ROLL ROOF COVERING
FOR FLAT ROOF

ROOF VENT

EXTERIOR WALL

PARAPET WALL

COCK LOFT

ROOF SHEATHING

METAL COUNTER FLASHING
OVER ROOF COVERING.
CHECK TO SEE CONDITION
AND IF ONE INSTALLED.

ROOF RAFTER

CEILING JOISTS

SPLASH BLOCK OR CONCRETE SLABS FOR PREVENTION OF RAIN RUN-OFF DOWN TO FOUNDATION WALLS

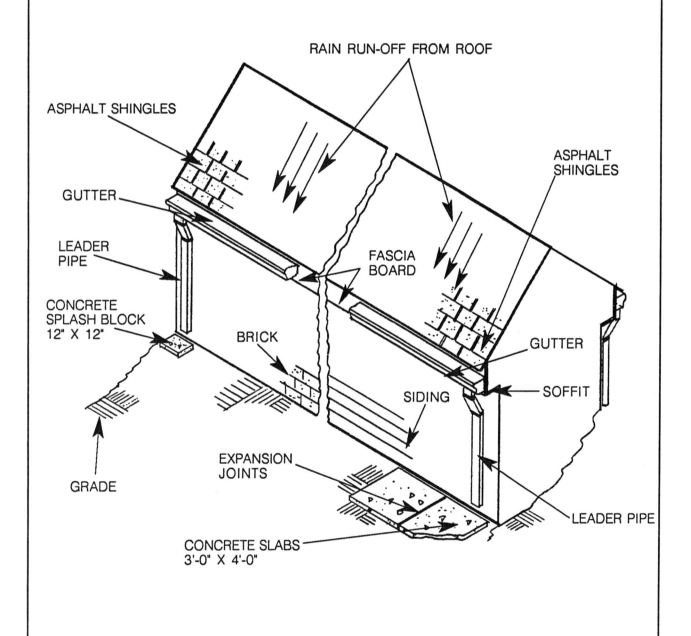

BALLOON-FRAME CONSTRUCTION

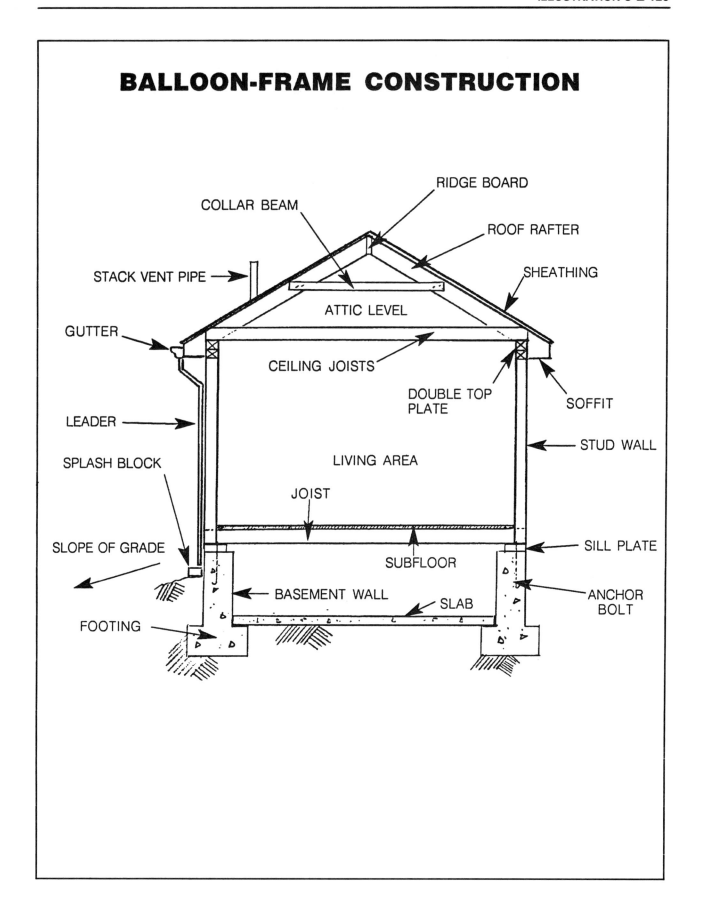

PLATFORM-FRAME CONSTRUCTION

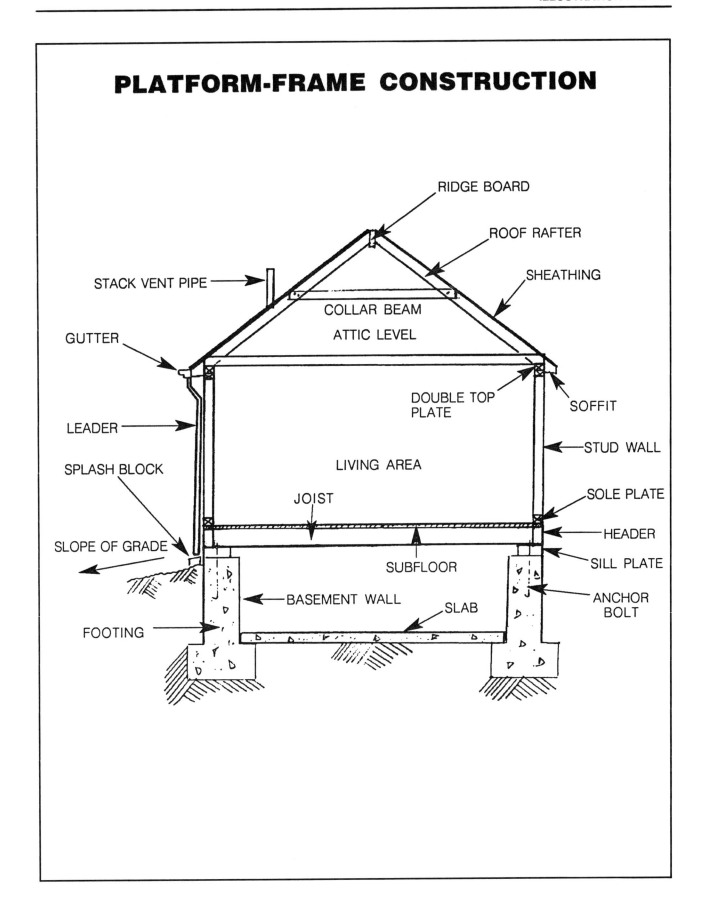

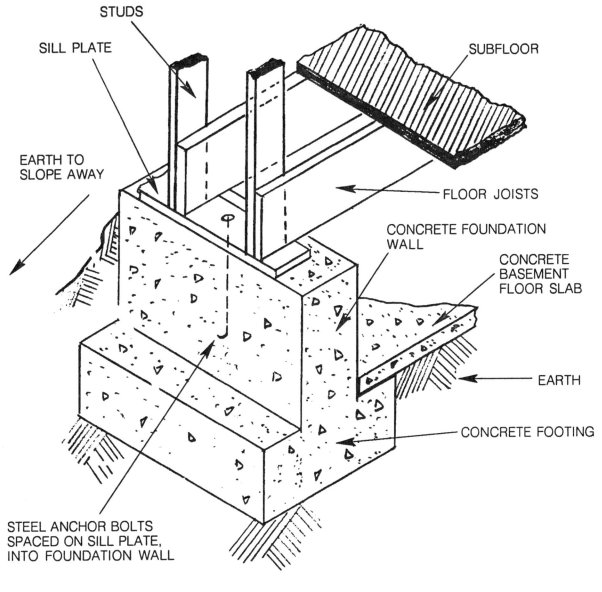

TYPICAL BALLOON-FRAME CONSTRUCTION SECTION VIEW

TYPICAL PLATFORM-FRAME CONSTRUCTION SECTION VIEW

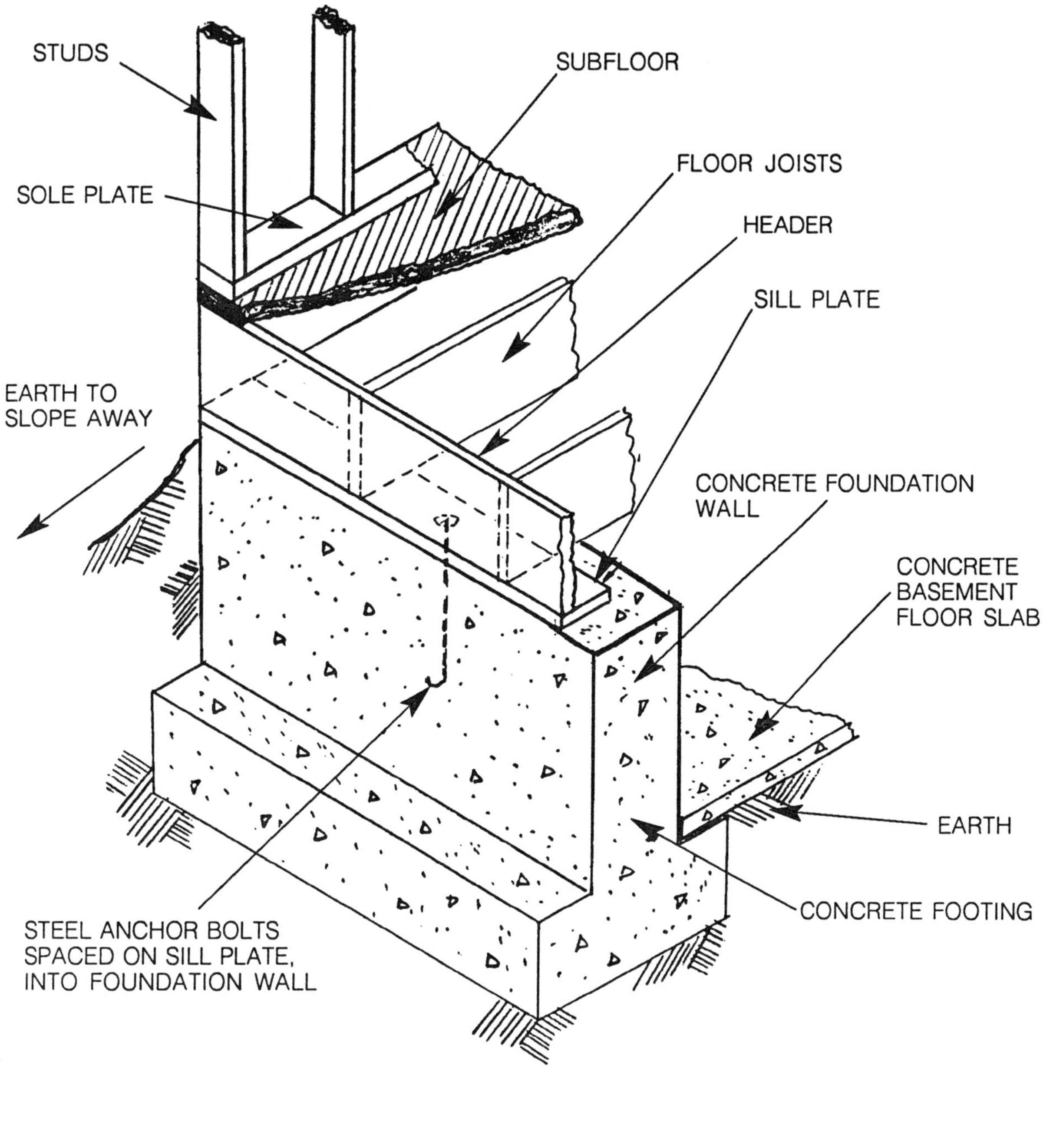

STUDS

SUBFLOOR

FLOOR JOISTS

SOLE PLATE

HEADER

SILL PLATE

EARTH TO SLOPE AWAY

CONCRETE FOUNDATION WALL

CONCRETE BASEMENT FLOOR SLAB

EARTH

CONCRETE FOOTING

STEEL ANCHOR BOLTS SPACED ON SILL PLATE, INTO FOUNDATION WALL

MAIN SUPPORT (WOOD OR STEEL) SUPPORTING FLOOR JOISTS

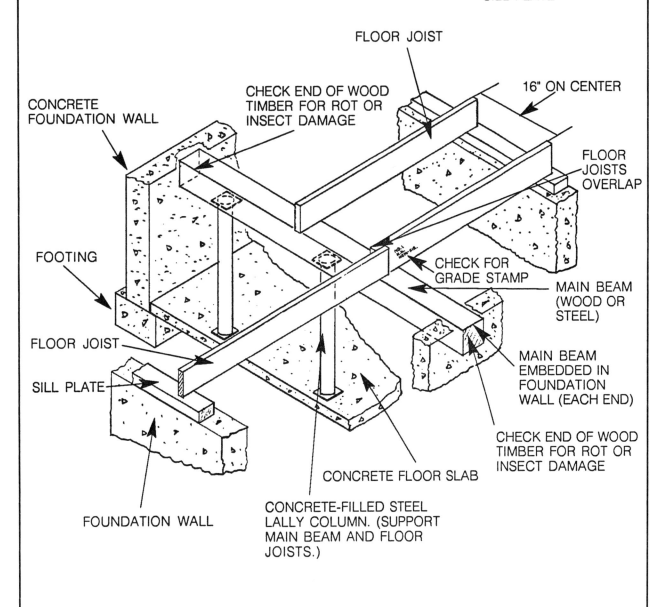

SILL PLATE

FLOOR JOIST

16" ON CENTER

CHECK END OF WOOD TIMBER FOR ROT OR INSECT DAMAGE

CONCRETE FOUNDATION WALL

FLOOR JOISTS OVERLAP

FOOTING

CHECK FOR GRADE STAMP

MAIN BEAM (WOOD OR STEEL)

FLOOR JOIST

MAIN BEAM EMBEDDED IN FOUNDATION WALL (EACH END)

SILL PLATE

CHECK END OF WOOD TIMBER FOR ROT OR INSECT DAMAGE

CONCRETE FLOOR SLAB

FOUNDATION WALL

CONCRETE-FILLED STEEL LALLY COLUMN. (SUPPORT MAIN BEAM AND FLOOR JOISTS.)

TYPICAL GABLE ROOF FRAMING

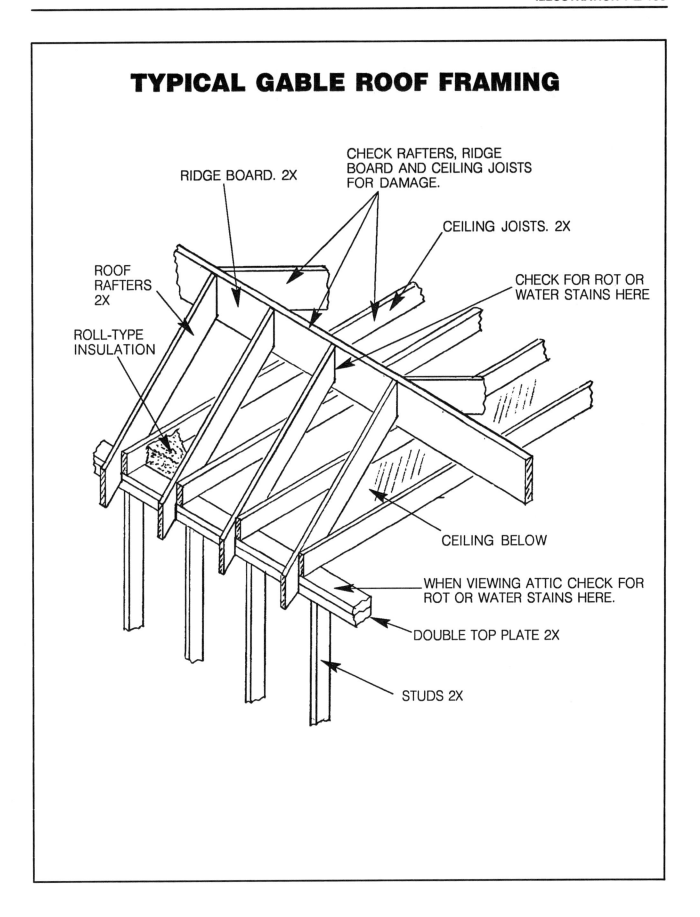

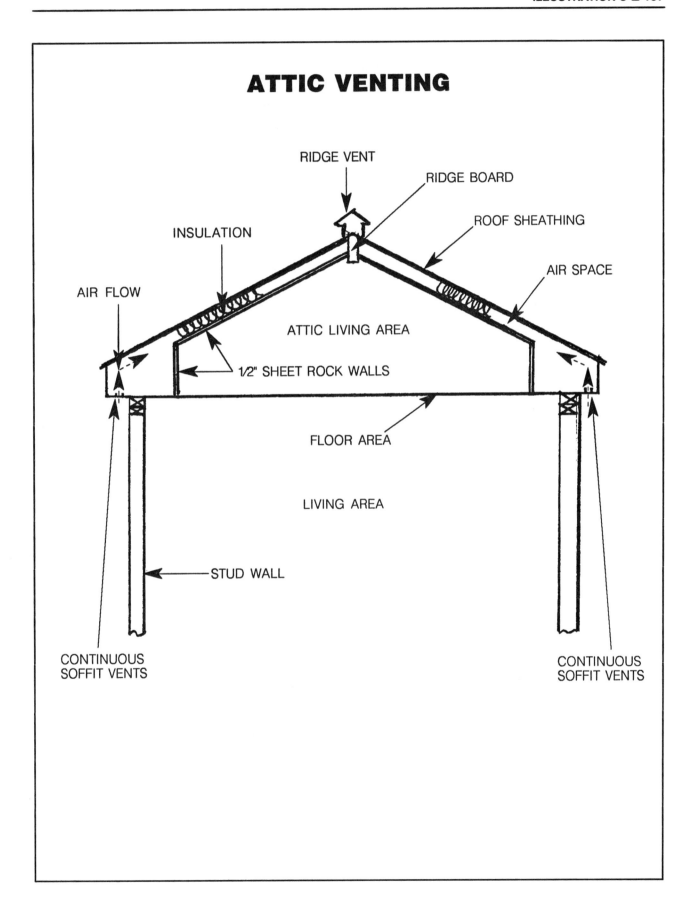

ILLUSTRATION V ■ 139

ENTRANCE STEPS

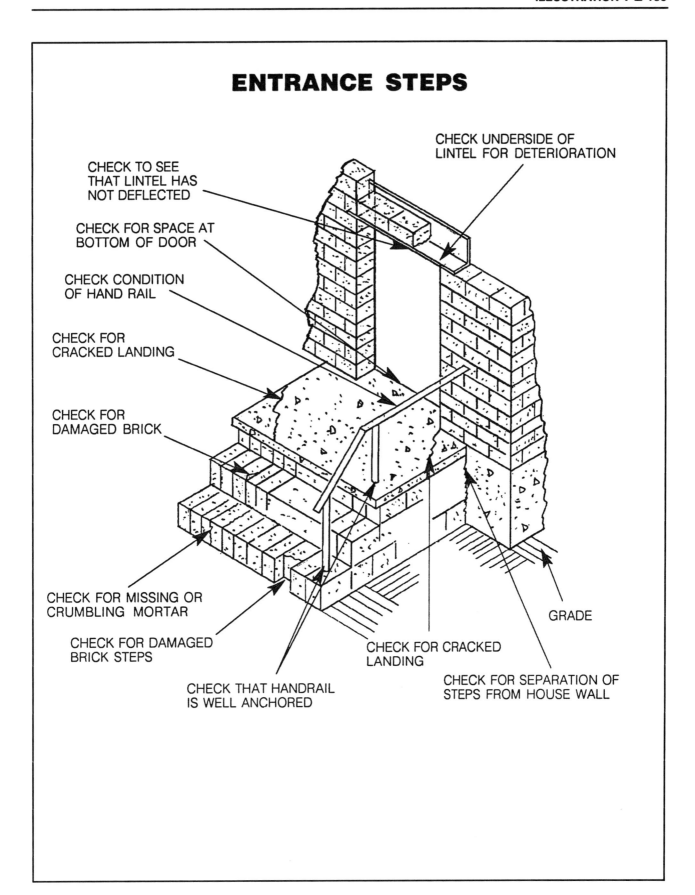

CHECK UNDERSIDE OF
LINTEL FOR DETERIORATION

CHECK TO SEE
THAT LINTEL HAS
NOT DEFLECTED

CHECK FOR SPACE AT
BOTTOM OF DOOR

CHECK CONDITION
OF HAND RAIL

CHECK FOR
CRACKED LANDING

CHECK FOR
DAMAGED BRICK

CHECK FOR MISSING OR
CRUMBLING MORTAR

CHECK FOR DAMAGED
BRICK STEPS

CHECK THAT HANDRAIL
IS WELL ANCHORED

CHECK FOR CRACKED
LANDING

GRADE

CHECK FOR SEPARATION OF
STEPS FROM HOUSE WALL

TERMITE INFESTATION OF FRAMING MEMBERS

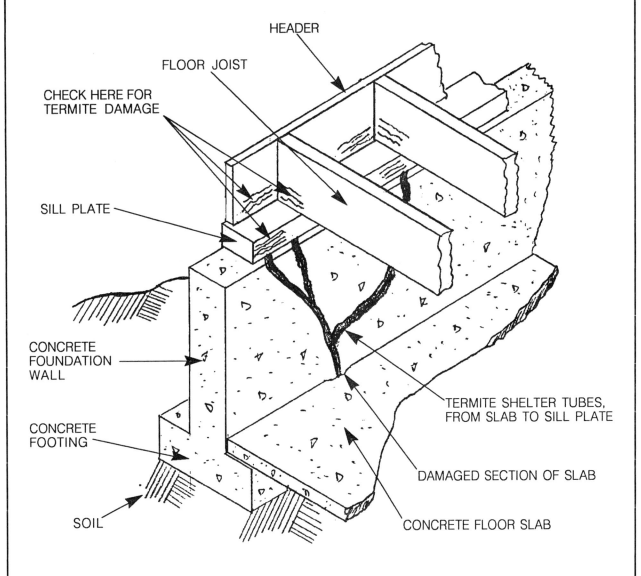

HEADER

FLOOR JOIST

CHECK HERE FOR TERMITE DAMAGE

SILL PLATE

CONCRETE FOUNDATION WALL

CONCRETE FOOTING

SOIL

TERMITE SHELTER TUBES, FROM SLAB TO SILL PLATE

DAMAGED SECTION OF SLAB

CONCRETE FLOOR SLAB

ILLUSTRATION X ■ 143

FREE-STANDING EXTERIOR CHIMNEY

TILE LINER

CHECK TO SEE IF CHIMNEY IS LEANING OVER ABOVE ROOF LINE

CHECK CAP FOR CRACKS

BRICK CHIMNEY

CHECK TO SEE IF CHIMNEY HAS FLASHING INSTALLED

CHECK CONDITION OF METAL FLASHING

STACK VENT

FASCIA BOARD. CHECK FOR DAMAGE.

BRICK EXTERIOR WALL

ASPHALT ROOF SHINGLES

CHECK MORTAR

CHECK JOINT BETWEEN CHIMNEY AND EXTERIOR WALL

GRADE

CHECK FOR LOOSE, MISSING MORTAR. ALSO CHECK FOR DAMAGED BRICK WORK.

CHECK JOINT BETWEEN CHIMNEY AND EXTERIOR WALL

CLEAN-OUT DOOR, OPEN IT AND INSPECT IT.

CHIMNEY FOOTING. BELOW GRADE.

TYPICAL STAIRCASE

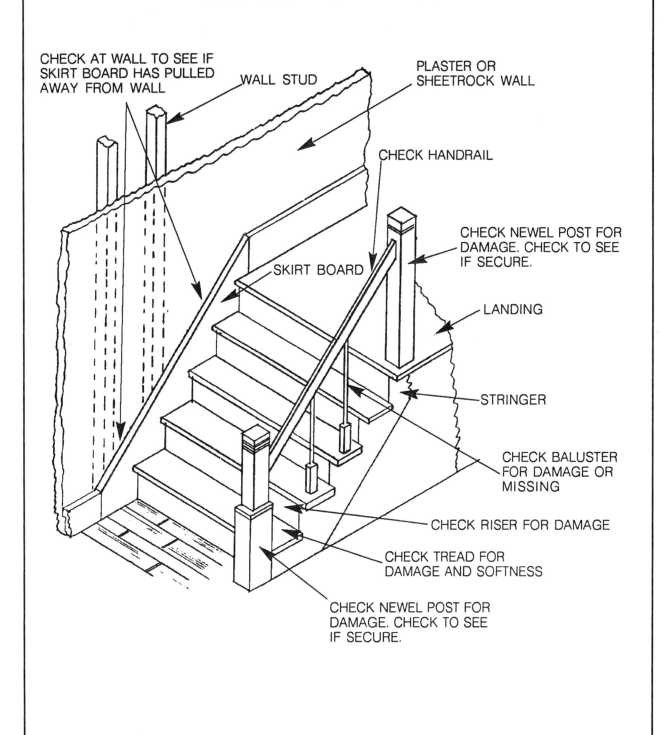

CHECK AT WALL TO SEE IF SKIRT BOARD HAS PULLED AWAY FROM WALL

WALL STUD

PLASTER OR SHEETROCK WALL

CHECK HANDRAIL

CHECK NEWEL POST FOR DAMAGE. CHECK TO SEE IF SECURE.

SKIRT BOARD

LANDING

STRINGER

CHECK BALUSTER FOR DAMAGE OR MISSING

CHECK RISER FOR DAMAGE

CHECK TREAD FOR DAMAGE AND SOFTNESS

CHECK NEWEL POST FOR DAMAGE. CHECK TO SEE IF SECURE.

LINTEL FAILURE OVER WINDOW

AS LINTEL DEFLECTS, THE BRICK
WORK IT IS SUPPORTING
BEGINS TO CRACK AND TEAR

LINTEL OVER WINDOW BEGINS
TO DEFLECT. THIS SHOWS
LINTEL IS BEGINNING TO FAIL.

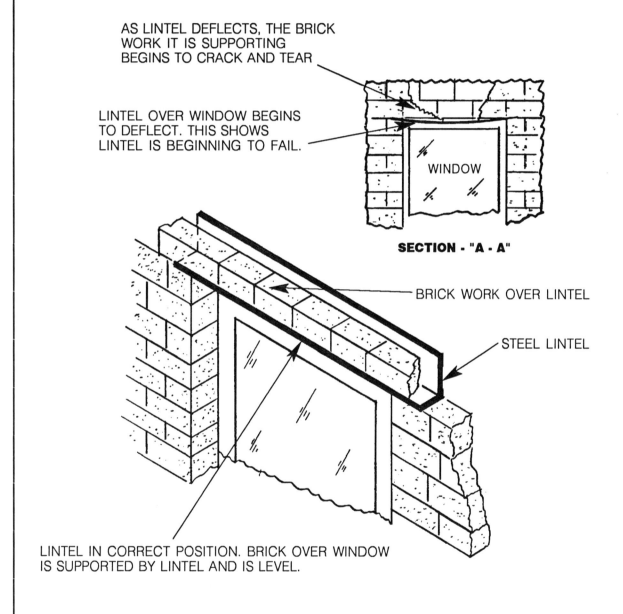

WINDOW

SECTION - "A - A"

BRICK WORK OVER LINTEL

STEEL LINTEL

LINTEL IN CORRECT POSITION. BRICK OVER WINDOW
IS SUPPORTED BY LINTEL AND IS LEVEL.

OLD BOILER CONVERTED TO OIL-FIRING

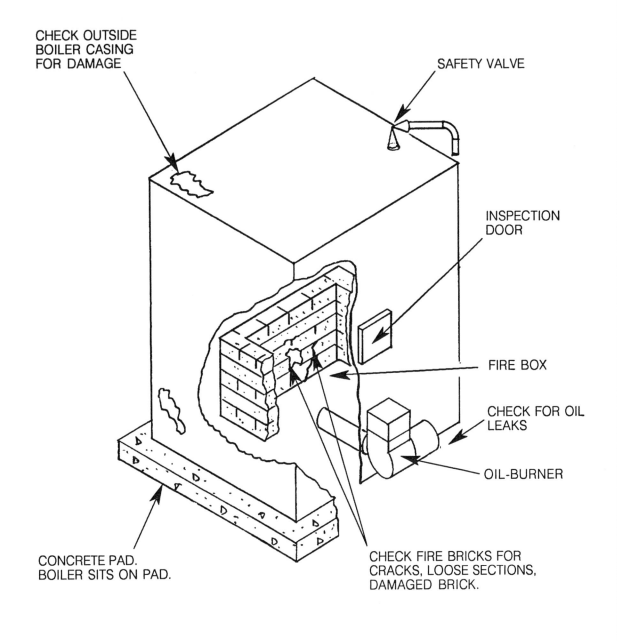

CHECK OUTSIDE BOILER CASING FOR DAMAGE

SAFETY VALVE

INSPECTION DOOR

FIRE BOX

CHECK FOR OIL LEAKS

OIL-BURNER

CONCRETE PAD. BOILER SITS ON PAD.

CHECK FIRE BRICKS FOR CRACKS, LOOSE SECTIONS, DAMAGED BRICK.

SCHEMATIC OF RADIANT FLOOR HEATING

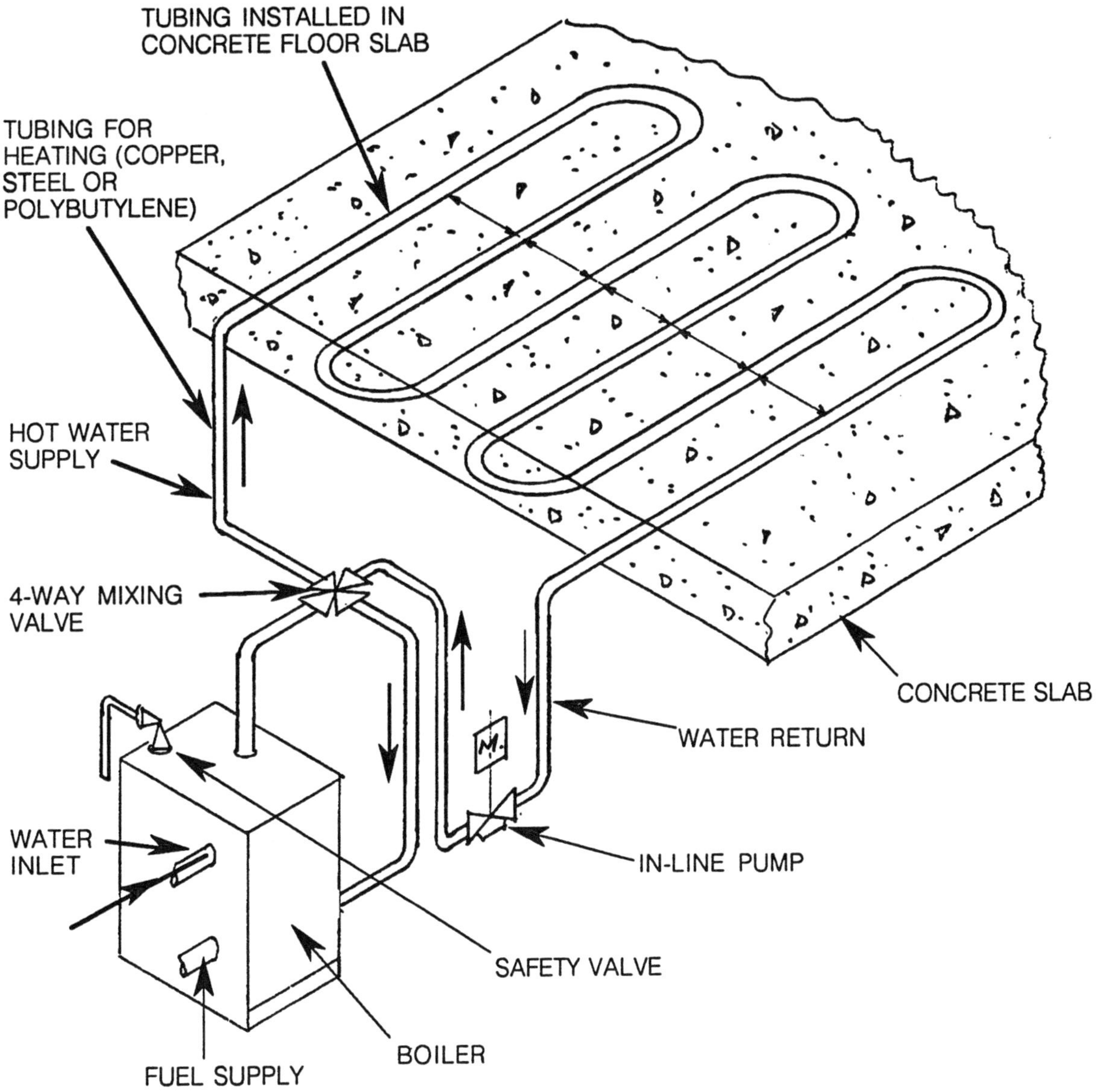

TUBING INSTALLED IN
CONCRETE FLOOR SLAB

TUBING FOR
HEATING (COPPER,
STEEL OR
POLYBUTYLENE)

HOT WATER
SUPPLY

4-WAY MIXING
VALVE

CONCRETE SLAB

WATER RETURN

IN-LINE PUMP

WATER
INLET

SAFETY VALVE

FUEL SUPPLY

BOILER

ILLUSTRATION CC ■ 153

BOILER WITH COIL FOR HOT WATER PRODUCTION

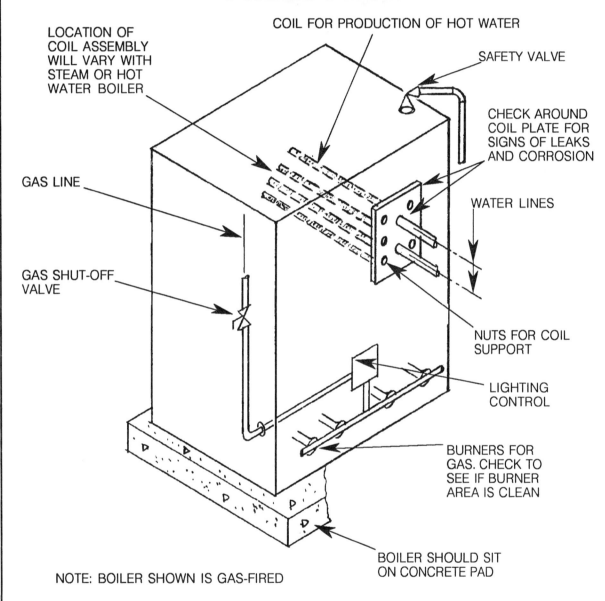

NOTE: BOILER SHOWN IS GAS-FIRED

BOILER WITH COIL FOR HOT WATER PRODUCTION

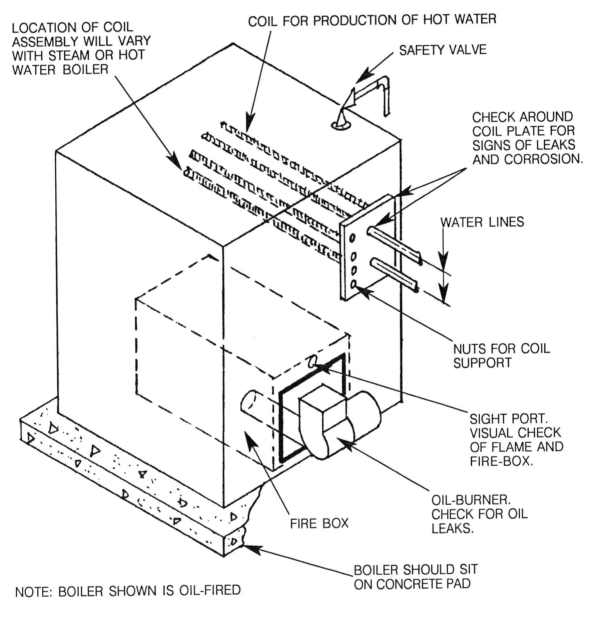

LOCATION OF COIL ASSEMBLY WILL VARY WITH STEAM OR HOT WATER BOILER

COIL FOR PRODUCTION OF HOT WATER

SAFETY VALVE

CHECK AROUND COIL PLATE FOR SIGNS OF LEAKS AND CORROSION.

WATER LINES

NUTS FOR COIL SUPPORT

SIGHT PORT. VISUAL CHECK OF FLAME AND FIRE-BOX.

OIL-BURNER. CHECK FOR OIL LEAKS.

FIRE BOX

BOILER SHOULD SIT ON CONCRETE PAD

NOTE: BOILER SHOWN IS OIL-FIRED

PARAPET WALL AND FLASHING

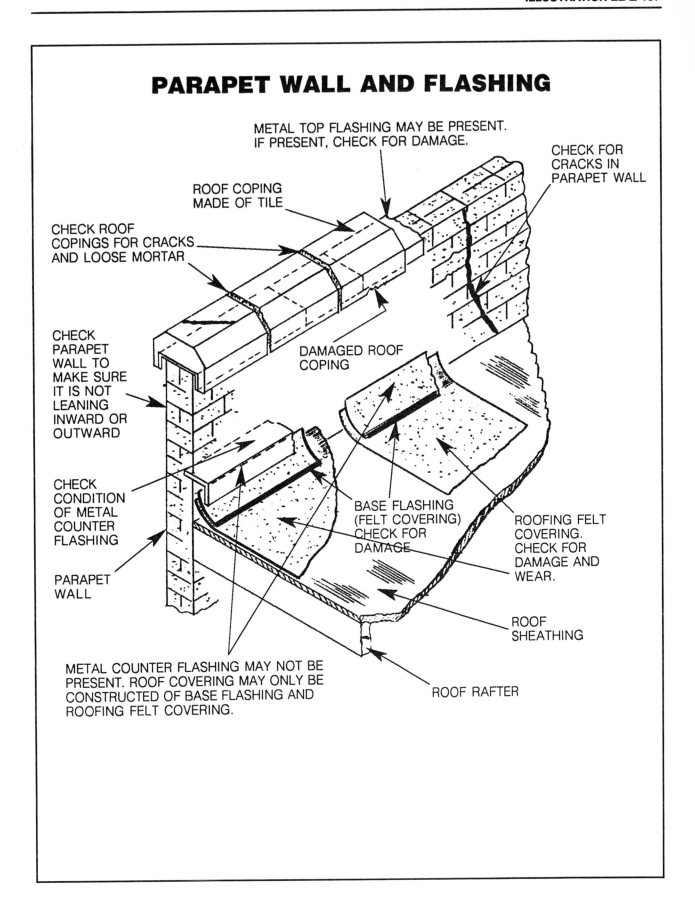

METAL TOP FLASHING MAY BE PRESENT. IF PRESENT, CHECK FOR DAMAGE.

CHECK FOR CRACKS IN PARAPET WALL

ROOF COPING MADE OF TILE

CHECK ROOF COPINGS FOR CRACKS AND LOOSE MORTAR

CHECK PARAPET WALL TO MAKE SURE IT IS NOT LEANING INWARD OR OUTWARD

DAMAGED ROOF COPING

CHECK CONDITION OF METAL COUNTER FLASHING

PARAPET WALL

BASE FLASHING (FELT COVERING) CHECK FOR DAMAGE

ROOFING FELT COVERING. CHECK FOR DAMAGE AND WEAR.

ROOF SHEATHING

METAL COUNTER FLASHING MAY NOT BE PRESENT. ROOF COVERING MAY ONLY BE CONSTRUCTED OF BASE FLASHING AND ROOFING FELT COVERING.

ROOF RAFTER

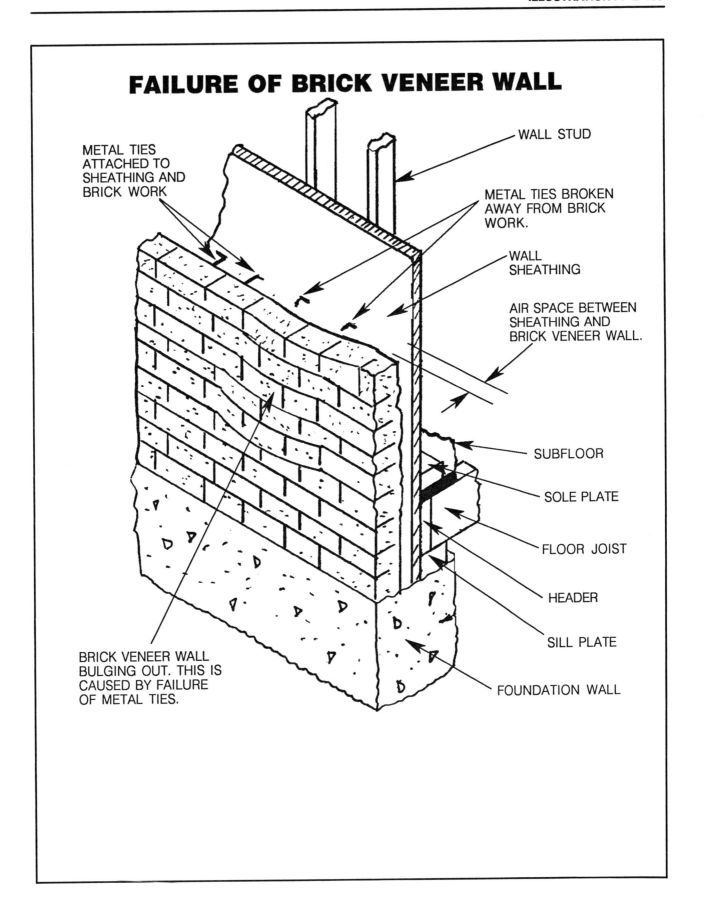

FAILURE OF BRICK VENEER WALL

WALL STUD

METAL TIES ATTACHED TO SHEATHING AND BRICK WORK

METAL TIES BROKEN AWAY FROM BRICK WORK.

WALL SHEATHING

AIR SPACE BETWEEN SHEATHING AND BRICK VENEER WALL.

SUBFLOOR

SOLE PLATE

FLOOR JOIST

HEADER

SILL PLATE

FOUNDATION WALL

BRICK VENEER WALL BULGING OUT. THIS IS CAUSED BY FAILURE OF METAL TIES.

REPLACEMENT OF STANDARD WINDOW WITH HIGH-ENERGY SAVING WINDOW

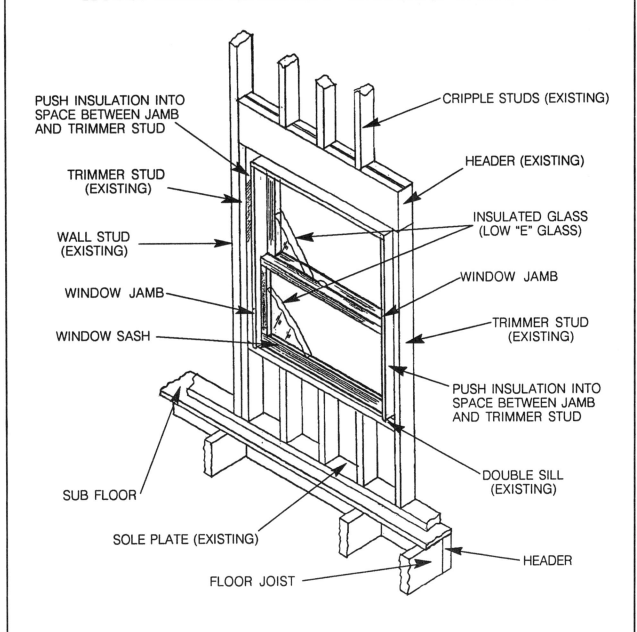

PUSH INSULATION INTO SPACE BETWEEN JAMB AND TRIMMER STUD

TRIMMER STUD (EXISTING)

WALL STUD (EXISTING)

WINDOW JAMB

WINDOW SASH

SUB FLOOR

SOLE PLATE (EXISTING)

FLOOR JOIST

CRIPPLE STUDS (EXISTING)

HEADER (EXISTING)

INSULATED GLASS (LOW "E" GLASS)

WINDOW JAMB

TRIMMER STUD (EXISTING)

PUSH INSULATION INTO SPACE BETWEEN JAMB AND TRIMMER STUD

DOUBLE SILL (EXISTING)

HEADER

FOUNDATION EVALUATION

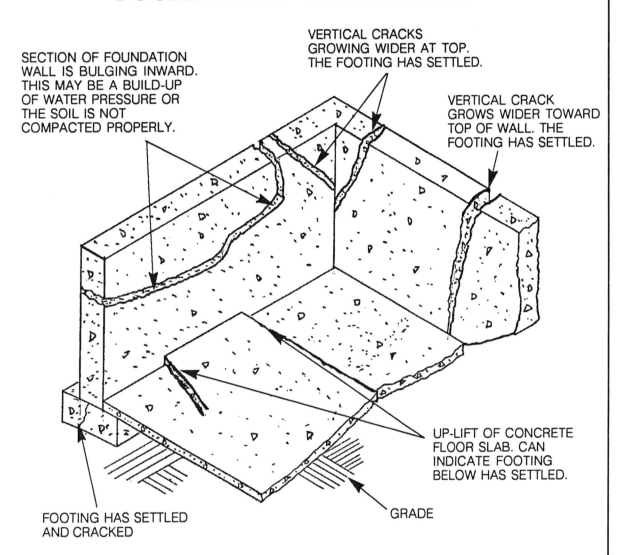

SECTION OF FOUNDATION WALL IS BULGING INWARD. THIS MAY BE A BUILD-UP OF WATER PRESSURE OR THE SOIL IS NOT COMPACTED PROPERLY.

VERTICAL CRACKS GROWING WIDER AT TOP. THE FOOTING HAS SETTLED.

VERTICAL CRACK GROWS WIDER TOWARD TOP OF WALL. THE FOOTING HAS SETTLED.

UP-LIFT OF CONCRETE FLOOR SLAB. CAN INDICATE FOOTING BELOW HAS SETTLED.

FOOTING HAS SETTLED AND CRACKED

GRADE

NOTE: IN OLD HOMES, IT IS NOT UNCOMMON TO SEE SMALL HAIRLINE CRACKS IN FOUNDATION WALLS. THE CRACKS AND SEPARATIONS DESCRIBED ABOVE ARE AT LEAST 1/4" AND WIDER.

FRAMING OF JOISTS AT FOUNDATION WALL (JOISTS SPAN WIDTH OF HOUSE)

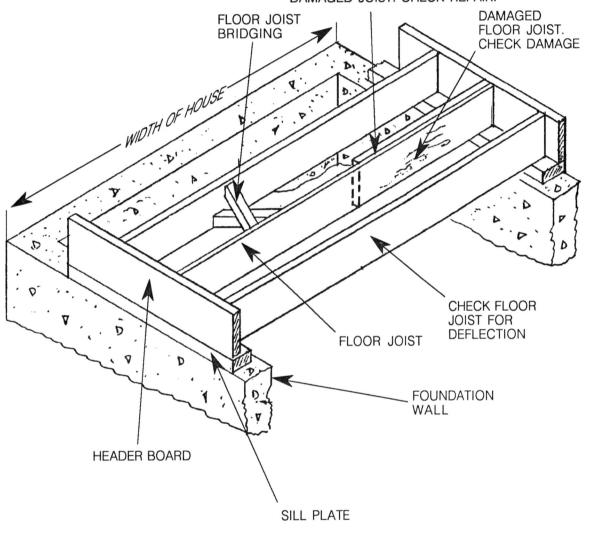

SECTION OF JOIST SISTERED TO DAMAGED JOIST. CHECK REPAIR.

FLOOR JOIST BRIDGING

DAMAGED FLOOR JOIST. CHECK DAMAGE

WIDTH OF HOUSE

CHECK FLOOR JOIST FOR DEFLECTION

FLOOR JOIST

FOUNDATION WALL

HEADER BOARD

SILL PLATE

CRAWL SPACE WITH VAPOR BARRIER

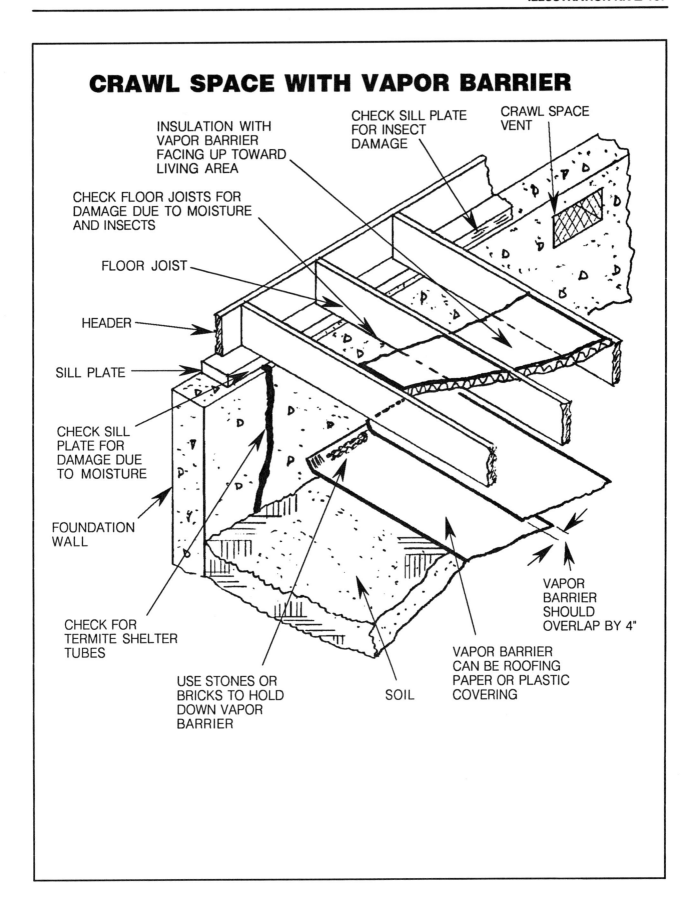

INSULATION WITH VAPOR BARRIER FACING UP TOWARD LIVING AREA

CHECK SILL PLATE FOR INSECT DAMAGE

CRAWL SPACE VENT

CHECK FLOOR JOISTS FOR DAMAGE DUE TO MOISTURE AND INSECTS

FLOOR JOIST

HEADER

SILL PLATE

CHECK SILL PLATE FOR DAMAGE DUE TO MOISTURE

FOUNDATION WALL

CHECK FOR TERMITE SHELTER TUBES

USE STONES OR BRICKS TO HOLD DOWN VAPOR BARRIER

SOIL

VAPOR BARRIER CAN BE ROOFING PAPER OR PLASTIC COVERING

VAPOR BARRIER SHOULD OVERLAP BY 4"

ILLUSTRATION LL ■ 169

ELECTRICAL BOX INSTALLATION FOR AIR CONDITIONING UNIT

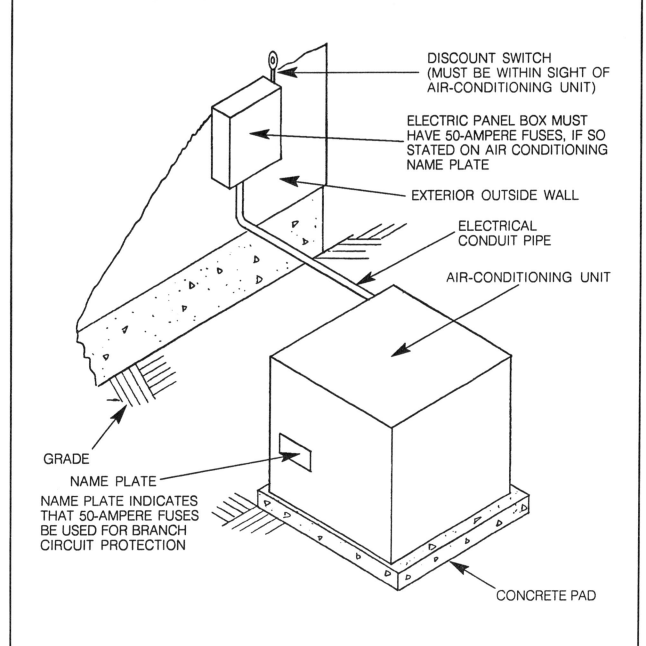

DISCOUNT SWITCH
(MUST BE WITHIN SIGHT OF
AIR-CONDITIONING UNIT)

ELECTRIC PANEL BOX MUST
HAVE 50-AMPERE FUSES, IF SO
STATED ON AIR CONDITIONING
NAME PLATE

EXTERIOR OUTSIDE WALL

ELECTRICAL
CONDUIT PIPE

AIR-CONDITIONING UNIT

GRADE

NAME PLATE

NAME PLATE INDICATES
THAT 50-AMPERE FUSES
BE USED FOR BRANCH
CIRCUIT PROTECTION

CONCRETE PAD

Index